Modern Language Association of America

Options for Teaching

Joseph Gibaldi, Series Editor

1. *Options for the Teaching of English: The Undergraduate Curriculum.* Edited by Elizabeth Wooten Cowan. 1975.
2. *Options for the Teaching of English: Freshman Composition.* Edited by Jasper P. Neel. 1978.
3. *Options for Undergraduate Foreign Language Programs: Four-Year and Two-Year Colleges.* By Renate A. Schulz. 1979.
4. *The Teaching Apprentice Program in Language and Literature.* Edited by Joseph Gibaldi and James V. Mirollo. 1981.
5. *Film Study in the Undergraduate Curriculum.* Edited by Barry Keith Grant. 1983.
6. *Part-Time Academic Employment in the Humanities: A Sourcebook for Just Policy.* Edited by M. Elizabeth Wallace. 1984.
7. *Teaching Environmental Literature: Materials, Methods, Resources.* Edited by Frederick O. Waage. 1985.
8. *School-College Collaborative Programs in English.* Edited by Ron Fortune. 1986.
9. *New Methods in College Writing Programs: Theories in Practice.* Edited by Paul Connolly and Teresa Vilardi. 1986.

New Methods in College Writing Programs
Theories in Practice

Edited by

Paul Connolly
and
Teresa Vilardi

The Modern Language Association of America
New York   1986

Copyright © 1986 by The Modern Language Association of America

Library of Congress Cataloging-in-Publication Data

New methods in college writing programs.

  (Options for teaching ; 9)
  Bibliography: p.
  Includes index.
  1. English language—Rhetoric—Study and teaching—
United States. I. Connolly, Paul H., 1942–
II. Vilardi, Teresa, 1943–   III. Series.
PE1405.U6N49 1986   808'.042'071273   86-16259
ISBN 0-87352-362-8
ISBN 0-87352-363-6 (pbk.)

Published by The Modern Language Association of America
10 Astor Place, New York, New York 10003

Contents

Acknowledgments	vii
Introduction	1
Paul Connolly	
1. Bard College	6
Teresa Vilardi	
2. Beaver College	12
Elaine P. Maimon	
3. Brooklyn College, City University of New York	16
Mary Oestereicher	
4. Brown University	21
Tori Haring-Smith	
5. Carnegie-Mellon University	26
David S. Kaufer	
6. Cornell University	29
Fredric V. Bogel	
7. Eastern Oregon State College	33
Lois Barry	
8. George Mason University	40
Marie Wilson Nelson	
9. Georgetown University	48
James F. Slevin	
10. Grinnell College	52
Mathilda Liberman	
11. Illinois State University	57
Janet Youga, Janice Neuleib, and Maurice Scharton	
12. Jackson State University	65
Allison Wilson	
13. La Salle University	71
Margot Soven	
14. Miami University	76
Mary Fuller and Donald A. Daiker	
15. Michigan Technological University	81
Diana L. George	
16. New York University	85
Lil Brannon	
17. St. Edward's University	89
John A. Perron, CSC	
18. State University of New York, Stony Brook	95
Peter Elbow and Pat Belanoff	
19. University of Maryland, College Park	106
Eugene Hammond	
20. University of Massachusetts, Amherst	111
Charles Moran	
21. University of Michigan, Ann Arbor	117
Patricia L. Stock	

22. University of Montevallo 122
    Dorothy G. Grimes
23. University of New Hampshire 130
    Gary H. Lindberg
24. University of Pittsburgh 135
    Paul J. Kameen
25. University of Utah 139
    Susan Miller
26. University of Washington 143
    Joan Graham
27. Western Kentucky University 149
    Karen Pelz
28. Whittier College 155
    William A. Geiger, Jr.

Works Cited 161

Topical Index 167

Acknowledgments

This book is a project of the Institute for Writing and Thinking at Bard College. After two summers' development of an intensive three-week workshop in language and thinking for its entering freshmen, Bard College, under the leadership of President Leon Botstein, established the Institute for Writing and Thinking in September 1982. The institute provides workshops, consultation, conferences, and publications to high school and college teachers who seek to improve interactive instruction in close reading, critical thinking, and clear writing in all courses. In the institute's first three years, over five thousand teachers from several hundred schools and colleges participated in five generations of workshops in teaching writing and thinking, writing in the social sciences, teaching critical inquiry, teaching poetry (reading and writing), and writing in the sciences and mathematics. These workshops are presented on the campuses of Bard and Simon's Rock colleges, through on-site consulting, and at conferences sponsored by the institute and other organizations.

This institute is made possible by grants from the AT&T, Apple, Booth Ferris, Ford, Exxon, Hazen, and Sprague foundations, and we gratefully acknowledge this support. All activities of the institute reflect the collective experience and generous collaboration of forty faculty associates, recruited nationally for their interest and experience in writing instruction, and we also gratefully acknowledge their work.

Paul Connolly, Director
Teresa Vilardi, Associate Director
Bard Institute for Writing and Thinking

Paul Connolly

Introduction

The first purpose of this book is to report new methods of teaching and administering college writing programs. These twenty-eight descriptions of recently revised programs reflect changes that are occurring throughout the country. Cumulatively, the essays provide what an ethnographer might call a "thick description" of the culture of our composition classrooms. They record and distinguish significant changes in the way writing is now taught and learned. Yes, these essays discuss the heuristic value of writing, writing centers, writing-intensive courses, and writing across the curriculum, but they are also about the behavior of teachers and students in a classroom, about the social dance of thought and language, and about systems of knowledge in a pluralistic democracy.

That is one purpose. A second is to emphasize that methods are replacing muddles. The daily practice of writing instruction is now generally informed by the rich theory and research of the past quarter century. Increasingly, writing classes are influenced not only by the writings of James Britton, Janet Emig, James Moffett, Peter Elbow, and Ann Berthoff, for example, but also by the thought of Lev S. Vygotsky on the development of concepts in children; Walter J. Ong and Shirley B. Heath on orality and literacy; Richard Rorty, Clifford Geertz, and Thomas S. Kuhn on the social authority of knowledge; Susanne K. Langer on the cognitive dimension of feeling. Writing, once the impoverished charge of the untenured, now commands the attention of many expert teachers and scholars. The "literacy crisis" has initiated a radical inquiry into learning, and these essays record not so much surface changes in teaching—another day's survival strategies—as emergent methods of learning: theories in practice.

If students need a sense of plenty, the rhetorician's *copia*, in order to compose, teachers and administrators require their own full sense of possibility to be creative. That is the final purpose of this book: to suggest what more or different might be done in writing programs. Readers looking to renovate their programs may find helpful models here. Those who are generally pleased with the operation of their programs may still find useful means of reviewing, perhaps refining, what they do. The authors of these essays are either the directors of the programs they describe or closely associated with those programs, and addresses are provided so that readers may request further information.

Many of the programs represented here enjoy a reputation established through published notices, conference presentations, or the admiration of professionals in the field. Others are included because their directors, responding to announcements of this project in professional journals, presented insightful reports from which others might learn. This collection makes no claim to single out all the imaginatively developing programs in the country or to commend those here, merely by virtue of their inclusion, as "most successful." Rather, our cumulative goal has been to suggest how writing programs are changing in response to the recent intensive analysis of the theory and practice of writing instruction.

Contributors were asked to describe certain aspects of their programs—general designs, historical development, theoretical assumptions that inform the teaching method(s), staffing and teacher training, strengths and problems—and to provide the data that precedes each essay. They were also invited, however, to focus on "distinctive features of the program, noting successful innovation or experimentation that might guide others."

We have not required essays to conform to one format, nor have we standardized the style or content of these presentations, preferring that each school represent itself as it judged best. The resultant reports may seem irregular at times, inconsistent in intention, voice, emphasis, and style. This is the irregularity of our profession, particularly in a transitional moment, and we have allowed, even encouraged diversity as an accurate reflection of how unevenly change occurs and of how it is determined by temperament and inclination as well as by method.

What is intended by the description of these programs as "innovative"? This book is, in a sense, a sequel to *Options for the Teaching of English: Freshman Composition*, edited by Jasper P. Neel. Neel's objective, however, was to present a "cross section of various approaches currently in use" (as of 1976), to provide "an overview of the ways different institutions deal with the teaching of writing" (v, vii), not to focus on "innovative" programs. Of the eighteen programs described, he classified ten as "traditional" in that they were designed for freshmen; required; housed in, and the sole responsibility of, the English department; and taught primarily (85%) by graduate students. "Nontraditional" programs shared the responsibility for writing instruction among various departments; offered upper-level as well as freshman writing courses; and provided such novelties as, in one instance, a televised composition program.

In the past decade, many college writing programs have deliberately moved away from the simple "assignment-product-rating" cycle of writing instruction, which emphasizes testing displayed knowledge, and toward what is generally called a "process" approach, which values writing as an instrument of learning. In the latter system, teachers support students through a multiple-draft revision of writing that is informed by reading, peer responses, and conferences and through probative writing that clarifies audience, purpose, and structure as thinking proceeds. This process approach has been influenced by numerous books and articles on writing instruction in the past fifteen years. Old practices do not fall easily into step with new precepts, however, and in 1983 Clinton S. Burhans, Jr., of Michigan State University, was dismayed to report, after a study of 263 college catalogs from fifty states, how little impact contemporary theory seemed to be having on traditional practice. "Surfing on the waves of books and articles dealing with theory, research, and application in writing . . . can be an exuberant experience," he wrote, but, when one observes writing teachers at work, "the sobering reality is how few seem to know the surf is up or even that there is a sea there at all" (639).

College catalogs may themselves be out of step with both practice and precept, but in any event, the following reports are cause for greater optimism. The organizing question behind this survey of writing programs has been: Who is teaching what, how, and why? The following elements in the answers given here are noteworthy:

(1) Many writing courses are still taught by graduate students, but these teachers are more thoroughly trained and supervised than in the past, through courses, staff meetings, and classroom observation. Further, more full-time faculty members are teaching writing. As Jasper Neel noted eight years ago, "teachers and administrators have begun to see the teaching of composition as an end in itself, not a temporary assignment on the way to bigger and better things" (v). Perhaps Mina Shaughnessy would have less cause now to lament the aversion of "belletrists" to composition courses than she did in *Errors and Expectations* (1977). At Beaver, Miami, Georgetown, and elsewhere, tenured and tenure-track teachers seem committed to improving writing instruction. writing instruction.

(2) Writing classes are still large, often exceeding twenty students, and Eugene Hammond of the University of Maryland speaks for many when he writes that "teaching two twenty-student courses each semester grinds away at a teaching assistant: it is more work than most people can perform with enthusiasm and still sustain interest in graduate school for more than two or three years." Workshops are becoming more common than lectures, however, and many schools seem to think of their writing classes as, in the words of Charles Moran (Massachusetts), "studio courses, in which students perform an activity under the supervision of a practitioner who has more experience in this activity than they do."

(3) The responsibility for writing instruction now often extends beyond the English department, as evidenced by the composition boards at Michigan or Pittsburgh, for example, or by the upper-level "writing intensive" courses in many schools.

(4) Fewer schools are exempting any students from a writing course; as at New York University, a placement exam may allow students to register in an honors or upper-level course, but writing instruction is deemed valuable for all students throughout college.

(5) Freshman English is becoming a writing course, in which the students' writing is the principal text. It is also, with increasing frequency, a reading course in which construing and constructing texts are taught, as Ann Berthoff urged in *The Making of Meaning*, as complementary instances of the imagination "making meaning." Where handbooks are used, they are treated as reference tools, not course syllabi.

(6) Written language is regarded as an instrument of learning appropriate to all courses. Exploratory, speculative writing is valued as a source of personal knowledge and as a means of engaging students actively in their education.

(7) The teaching of basic writing is also changing, as teachers move from drill-and-skill remediation to more intensive instruction in sections that are methodologically similar to general writing courses. At Illinois State, Georgetown, or Pittsburgh, for example, emphasis is more broadly on reclamation than on remediation of "at-risk" students.

(8) Many of the programs described here work to develop collaborative learning within communities—a writing community, a teaching community, and a general learning community that may employ peer tutors as valued contributors to the educational process. Gary Lindberg (New Hampshire) and Allison Wilson (Jackson State) speak eloquently of the importance of supporting responsibility and autonomy among students and teachers. Tori Haring-

Smith (Brown) describes one peer-tutoring program that, like others mentioned here, values such ends.

(9) Individual programs have distinctive emphases—problem solving at Carnegie-Mellon, sentence combining at Miami, linguistic theory at Whittier, or conferencing at New Hampshire—in part attributable to the leadership on these campuses. Yet most administrators recognize the need to integrate what James Britton in *The Development of Writing Abilities* has termed "expressive" and "transactional" writing, in order to promote engaged writing and thinking. It is not always clear when a balance is struck, as evidenced by the differing reports from, for example, Western Kentucky, Georgetown, Jackson State, and Massachusetts. Charles Moran (Massachusetts) writes, "It is the program's belief that most students coming to the university can handle descriptive and narrative writing, particularly of the autobiographical kind. The students have more difficulty, however, in working with abstractions." Karen Pelz (Western Kentucky) maintains that her students need "to begin at what Britton calls the expressive level or what others might call the personal essay, essentially narrative and descriptive in mode and based on personal experience." Where they would no doubt agree is on the need to nurture confidence and fluency while extending what Lev Vygotsky called the student's "zone of proximal development."

(10) Comprehensive programs now often include writing centers and tutorial services, as well as a range of optional courses to fulfill a requirement, thereby acknowledging various learning needs and problems.

(11) There is increasing evidence of collaboration between preuniversity and university teachers. In programs at Bard (the Institute for Writing and Thinking), Miami, George Mason (both sites of the National Writing Project), Michigan, and Georgetown, for example, secondary and college teachers combine their knowledge and experience so that writing is not fragmented into "language arts," "the five-paragraph theme," and "higher-order reasoning."

(12) Many schools have initiated writing-proficiency tests. Peter Elbow and Pat Belanoff (SUNY, Stony Brook) describe an alternative "portfolio" assessment that makes testing a part of, not an appendage to, learning. Other large institutions (notably, the University of Massachusetts, Amherst) also require formative evaluation by students of their work through portfolios.

(13) Most programs described are the product of revision in the past five years—often as part of a general curricular reform. One detects at work here institutional commitments to improving writing and an awareness of the centrality of language in learning. But change does not come about easily, as reports from Montevallo, Western Kentucky, La Salle, Eastern Oregon, or Maryland bear witness. These schools and others must be sensitive to different styles of teaching and learning, as well as to the need to seek improvements without imposing a monolithic method on an institution.

(14) In *Writing in the Secondary School* Arthur Applebee of Stanford University recommended "Creating contexts in which writing serves... natural purposes" but called this recommendation "the most difficult to implement" (105). Program directors at Washington, Maryland, Massachusetts, and elsewhere testify to the importance and difficulty of this goal, for as Charles Moran writes, "outside the academy the writer can easily discover audience, voice, and purpose. Inside the academy the situation is substantially artificial and much less clear, particularly in a non- or pandisciplinary freshman

course." To a certain extent, the schooling environment itself contributes to a lack of authentic discourse, a problem with which many programs are still wrestling.

Despite such difficulties the influence of James Britton, Janet Emig, Ann Berthoff, James Moffett, Donald Murray, Peter Elbow, and other researchers and theorists alluded to throughout these essays is having a practical impact on writing programs, at both the college and secondary levels. None of the programs described here is without continuing problems, as their directors acknowledge frankly. And even two dozen swallows do not a summer make. But a healthy revision of writing instruction within the larger context of general education seems well advanced in many areas of the country. If these models further demonstrate what is possible and spare teachers and students some unnecessary trials and errors, they contribute to that new vision.

Teresa Vilardi

1. Bard College
Freshman Workshop in Language and Thinking

1. **Department responsible for the writing program:** Institute for Writing and Thinking

2. **Staffing**

Percentage of freshman composition courses taught by part-time faculty members	0%
Percentage taught by graduate students	0%
Percentage taught by full-time instructors	0%
Percentage taught by assistant, associate, and full professors	100%
Percentage taught by full-time members of departments other than English	30%

3. **Enrollment policy**

    Maximum enrollment   12
    Minimum enrollment   8
    Average enrollment   11

4. **Program size**

    Number of students enrolled in the freshman composition program
    summer 1983   230

    Number of sections of freshman composition offered
    summer 1983   20

Since 1981, Bard College's freshmen have arrived on campus in August, three weeks before the beginning of the fall semester, for an intensive writing program—the Freshman Workshop in Language and Thinking—that is required of all entering students and optional for transfers. Bard's president, Leon Botstein, initiated the workshop because he and other members of the Bard faculty were concerned that even students who wrote grammatically and syntactically correct papers often wrote without engagement, in language that was inauthentic. It was also clear that poor papers frequently resulted from inattentive reading of texts. Since Bard's rigorous liberal arts curriculum depends to a great extent on the students' writing and reading abilities, President Botstein decided to address the problem before the students had even begun classes.

He invited Peter Elbow, author of *Writing without Teachers* and *Writing with Power*, to develop a language program for the incoming class that would go beyond remedial concerns to address the important connections among reading, writing, and thinking. In spring 1981 Elbow began to collaborate with twenty writing teachers, shaping what would become the Bard Freshman Workshop in Language and Thinking. The teachers came to Bard from fourteen different colleges and universities to plan the first summer workshop. Bard faculty members were excluded from the first group of Language and Thinking teachers so that freshmen might benefit from and enjoy the workshop without worrying that their performance would influence faculty attitudes toward them once the regular academic semester began. When the workshop began in August 1981, Elbow, the twenty teachers, and the 240 students were all new to Bard College.

Although the specific content of the workshop has changed in emphasis since the first year, the original design and the philosophical assumptions that underlie it remain. We assume that an important reason for students' inability to write coherently and effectively is that they lack experience in thinking through their own words. They are so concerned with producing a finished product, with "getting the answer right," that they overlook the writing process and rarely use writing to help them discover what they think. Elbow deliberately selected faculty members who were interested in approaches to the teaching of writing that examined the writing process itself. Teachers in the Bard workshop believe that the more students use writing informally for exploration, discovery, and reflection, the more invested they become in all writing. To gain control over their writing, students need to have something to say. They need an opportunity to take intellectual risks in a supportive environment where response is constructive and where they are encouraged to generate a lot of material before attempting to revise and edit. The three-week program provides such an environment.

During the summer workshop, Bard freshmen meet in classes of ten to twelve students, five days a week for six hours and on Saturday morning for two hours. Each weekday consists of three workshops that focus on invention, reading, and responding to writing. Students are introduced to freewriting, process writing, and revision strategies intended to help them experience a "sense of plenty." Classes begin each morning with freewriting and directed freewriting. Students and teachers write together, at first without response. Students are neither required to read nor called on. But the atmosphere encourages students to read their writing aloud, and most contribute often. Experimenting with a variety of strategies for getting words on paper, students are invited to write in response to a broad topic or to a particular story, poem, essay, or photograph. Writing is also often used in class to encourage, enliven, or focus class discussions. Homework consists of completing a draft of a piece begun in class or preparing a text to be considered in class the next day.

Once they have produced many pieces of writing, students learn how to use other people's responses to shape their work. Collaborating in small groups, students listen closely to one another's written drafts, giving intelligent, constructive response. The kind of response depends on where the writer is in the writing process. When a piece of writing has no clear direction or form, students may limit their response to pointing out what words or phrases they liked, what the writer seems to be saying, and so on. Later on, when the writer begins to see an essay or story taking shape, students respond more specifically to the ideas expressed in the piece, how the argument develops or what is implied or needs to be further explored.

Two purposes are served here. First, students learn how to listen attentively to one another. Second, giving and receiving response to a piece of writing impresses upon students that writing is a process; that it evolves over time; and that an essay, story, or poem goes through several stages and revisions before it is finished. Each week they are responsible for completing a critical essay, a piece of fiction or poetry, and one other piece of nonfictional writing. These finished pieces are collected in a portfolio, which is reviewed by a faculty member in conferences throughout the program. At the end each teacher writes a letter assessing how the student's writing has developed and where it needs to go. The three-week program is otherwise ungraded.

Reading and Writing

Another important assumption of the program is that careful reading and clear, effective writing are interdependent, particularly for students entering Bard's liberal arts curriculum. The program therefore spends considerable time in reading, and responding to, a wide variety of texts drawn from literature, social studies, the arts, and the natural sciences. Texts of varying degrees of difficulty are selected by the workshop faculty and collected in an anthology printed each summer. In addition, teachers often make use of visual "texts" from current exhibits at Bard's art gallery. Working as a whole or in smaller groups, students render written texts aloud, experimenting with different voices, and spend time at an exhibit in the art gallery. Our objective here is to encourage students to attend carefully to the words of a text, and to notice the details of a drawing or photograph. Response to texts is first of all written, so that students begin to use writing to explore a text, to reflect on their own responses to what is said and unsaid, to raise questions, and to indicate ambiguities and difficulties. The Bard workshop makes it difficult for students to respond only to directives from faculty or to "write to please the teacher." The goal of the workshop is to foster the spirit of critical inquiry necessary for undertaking academic work at Bard and particularly for appreciating the various ways that academic disciplines use language and perceive the world.

The dual emphasis on reading and writing allows students to go directly into the Freshman Seminar Program once the three-week workshop is completed. The fall seminar focuses on the civilization of fifth-century Athens, the spring on nineteenth-century Europe. Students are asked to read carefully many difficult texts and to write seven short critical papers each semester. Several faculty members who teach the freshman seminar have also taught in the summer workshop. Their experience in the workshop affects the way they approach the material in the seminar, providing continuity between the presemester program and Bard's regular academic curriculum.

Peer Tutoring

A peer tutoring program became an integral part of the freshman workshop in 1982. Ten upper-level Bard students, selected by faculty nomination and student recommendation, are available to tutor freshmen who have special difficulties during the three-week workshop. Tutors are assigned to sections and attend classes, so freshmen get to know them. By now, any Bard student selected as a peer tutor will have participated in the freshman workshop and will be familiar with the approach. Tutors meet regularly as a group and with the workshop faculty to talk about peer tutoring, special problems of helping a student write a paper, and special problems encountered in tutoring. During the year peer tutors are available, on a drop-in basis or by appointment, to offer any student assistance in writing papers. Most students who request tutoring are freshmen, but over the last two years a greater number of upper-division students have sought the help of peer tutors. By this time, of course, nearly all students enrolled at Bard have taken the Freshman Workshop in Language and Thinking. They are more likely to write several drafts of a paper and to consult with a peer tutor.

Faculty Preparation

As the preceding description makes clear, a special feature of the Bard freshman program is the workshop model on which it is based. Students and faculty together form a community of writers. The way the faculty members work together to shape the freshman program reflects the workshop as a whole. They first meet in February, to review the summer's work, and then again in June to plan the next August workshop. Teachers also meet two evenings a week during the three-week program, and writing instruction is a constant subject of discussion throughout. Teachers often get together informally to provide support for one another; to share ideas; and to model various strategies for generating, responding to, or revising student writing. Unlike instructors who teach in a single department or a single college, the Bard workshop faculty members live and work in Boston, New York, Pennsylvania, Maryland, or Maine; they teach at community colleges, small liberal arts colleges, and state universities. But they maintain contact throughout the year by phone and mail, exchanging ideas and sharing writing.

Of the twenty instructors who began teaching in the workshop in 1981, thirteen have continued working in the program, including the current director, Paul Connolly. Since 1981 ten members of the Bard faculty have been part of the freshman workshop faculty; in 1984, four taught in the program, representing the departments of history, literature, anthropology, and philosophy. All the Bard faculty members in the freshman workshop teach in Bard's freshman seminar and have had the opportunity to incorporate workshop approaches into their seminar classes during the regular academic year.

Problems

The Bard workshop has had its problems and limitations, which might make it difficult to replicate at other colleges and universities. First, it is expensive: students are not charged any additional fees or tuition for the three-week program. In addition, those who teach in the program receive a stipend plus room and board for the three weeks, as well as small stipends for attending the planning meetings in February and June. The program also requires the campus to be ready for new students three weeks earlier than it had traditionally opened, and the staff of the dean of students (including the director of physical education, the campus food service, and peer counselors) must all begin their programs earlier. Colleges interested in adapting the Bard workshop but inhibited from doing so by the potential costs might consider shortening the length of the program to one or two weeks; they would have to do so carefully, of course, since the impact of the workshop depends on its intensity. They might also consider using their own faculty, a choice that might require some faculty development, perhaps in the summer preceding the workshop or during a winter break. Use of a college's own faculty, of course, has the advantage of encouraging integration of the program into the regular academic curriculum.

In addition to being expensive, the Bard workshop is demanding of the students' and the faculty's energy. Immediately after it ends, freshmen register for classes and faculty members return to full-time teaching positions, at their own institutions or at Bard. Two years ago Bard instituted a reading period during Thanksgiving break to give students and staff a chance to catch up on work and rest. In spite of the demands of the workshop, though, students have overwhelmingly recommended that it be continued. The instructors have found that their experience in the program regenerated their energy and rekindled their interest in both teaching and writing.

Workshop faculty members also struggled throughout the program with the inevitable tension that developed between their commitment to the writing process and the requirement that students produce a portfolio of finished pieces within three weeks. The objective of the summer workshop is to make students active learners, to give them enough time and support to develop a piece of writing in their own voice. But the need to produce finished pieces must also be acknowledged in a program that prepares students to enter the academic communities of discourse. Fortunately, the small class size in the Bard program allows the faculty to pay special attention to students who are experiencing difficulty in producing finished pieces. At a larger institution, where it might not be possible to give students such individual attention, greater use of a peer tutoring program would probably be useful.

Strengths

Besides its success in improving reading and writing, the freshman workshop has served several other important functions, both intramurally and extramurally. For example, the workshop has become the focus for a unique orientation to college, although this was not its original intent. It serves as an introduction to the intellectual life of the college and to college-level work. In addition, the workshop has incidentally provided a context for the social orientation to the college. The dean of students is responsible for planning activities, social events, and general orientation to the college and the local community. But the workshop's emphasis on collaborative learning in small groups, its community readings, peer tutoring program, and use of the college facilities for writing assignments not only help students become accustomed to Bard and to college life but also foster the growth of mutual respect and cooperation within the entering class.

Another unique aspect of the Freshman Workshop in Language and

Thinking is the opportunity it offers the faculty to come together, as a group of writers and teachers, to share insights and ideas about the writing process and the teaching of writing. For this reason the freshman workshop is like an experimental laboratory for new approaches to teaching writing. As such, it has attracted the attention of writing teachers all over the country who were interested in knowing more about successful approaches to teaching writing and thinking. In 1982 Bard established the Institute for Writing and Thinking in response to the interest from the educational community. Funded by the Booth Ferris, Exxon, and Ford foundations, the institute offers consultation and workshops, modeled on those provided for Bard freshmen, to high school and college teachers in all disciplines. The institute is staffed by a director, an associate director, and twenty-five faculty associates. All institute faculty members must have previously taught, or must currently teach, in the Bard Freshman Workshop in Language and Thinking. In this way, they bring their experience with students to the work they do with teachers. The institute offers six two-day workshops for high school and college teachers during the academic year and week-long workshops in June. In addition, faculty associates of the institute give on-site consulting workshops at schools and colleges throughout the country. As of August 1985 the institute had offered forty workshops on the Bard and Simon's Rock campuses and sixty consulting workshops for four thousand teachers in all disciplines. Teachers who have participated in these workshops have appreciated the rare opportunity to write for and with their colleagues in an atmosphere of cooperation, support, and mutual exchange of ideas.

The Bard Freshman Workshop in Language and Thinking is now administered by the institute, whose director, Paul Connolly, is also the director of the freshman workshop. The institute is part of the Bard College Center, the public arm of the college, whose extensive activities include instituting national programs that encourage cooperation between secondary and post-secondary educators.

Elaine P. Maimon

2. Beaver College Writing Program

1. **Department responsible for the writing program:** English

2. **Staffing**

Percentage of freshman composition courses taught by part-time faculty members	20%
Percentage taught by graduate students	0–10%
Percentage taught by full-time instructors	0–10%
Percentage taught by assistant, associate, and full professors	60–80%
Percentage taught by full-time members of departments other than English	0–10%

3. **Enrollment policy**

   Maximum enrollment   20
   Minimum enrollment   15
   Average enrollment   18–19

4. **Program size**

   Number of students enrolled in the freshman composition program
   fall 1983   247
   spring 1984   228

   Number of sections of freshman composition offered
   fall 1983   13
   spring 1984   12

Theoretical Assumptions

Five principles shape the writing program at Beaver College:

1. Writing, like learning, is not an entity but a process.
2. Writing is a way to learn, not merely a means of communicating to others what has already been mastered.
3. Because writing and learning are interactive processes, students need instruction and practice in cooperating to learn from one another.
4. Because the writing within a discipline defines and manifests fundamental processes within the discipline, the teaching of writing is the responsibility of every scholar in every field.

5. Writing in each discipline is a form of social behavior in that discipline. Students must learn the conventions of aim and audience in each discipline, and they must also learn to control the common conventional features of the written code: spelling, punctuation, conformity to standard English usage.

Clearly, the philosophy of our program has been influenced most by the work of Mina Shaughnessy, Kenneth Bruffee, and James Kinneavy. Shaughnessy has taught us that our students' errors often reflect their innocence about the way writers behave and that it is our job to model for them the processes of writing and revising. Bruffee has taught us that we can best teach these processes through collaborative learning. Kinneavy has taught us that by assigning extended projects in draft stages and working with students at every stage to define aim and audience, faculty members in all disciplines can improve the teaching of their own subject matter as well as help to teach writing. Beaver College implements these philosophical principles through the teaching of writing in all college courses and through a freshman composition program, a writing center, and a graduate program in the teaching of writing. The result is a comprehensive, connected approach to writing and learning in all courses at all levels.

Freshman Composition at Beaver

Entering students take two semesters of composition, English 101 and 102. Because students will build throughout their college years on processes the course teaches, no one is exempt. On the basis of a two-part writing assignment completed by all freshmen during the orientation period, approximately fifteen percent of the freshman class is also placed in English 100, Basic Writing. English 100, like English 101 and 102, carries full academic credit for graduation. So, in effect, our weakest students are required to take three semesters of composition.

The freshman composition course is designed to introduce writing processes; to teach collaborative learning, including how to share drafts of work in progress; to exemplify elements of writing through a brief cross-disciplinary reading list; and to provide opportunities for practice in the conventions of standard written English. Each year the composition staff agrees on a prospectus that records our general operating principles along with a list of common readings and experiences. Within those boundaries, individual instructors can design their own syllabi. All staff members assign some reading in the natural and social sciences, as well as in the humanities; all instructors require students to write at least a thousand words per week, though the instructors grade only four finished papers; all assign the same grammar handbook and teach students to use it as a reference tool; all devote some class time to procedures for library research, including explicit instruction in summarizing and paraphrasing. The class is usually conducted as a writing workshop, although some time is devoted to discussions and short lectures. Attendance and consistent writing practice at the thousand-word-per-week minimum are strict requirements. Any student who misses class or fails to write the minimum amount for the equivalent of three weeks is dropped from the course. The composition program teaches processes; a student cannot pass simply by submitting the four finished products. We believe that most student writing that looks inadequate is really unfinished, and we are committed to teaching students how to finish their work.

We coordinate at least one of the four major writing projects with an assignment in another freshman course such as political science, psychology, or biology, and we encourage students to share drafts of their papers on a political candidate or on the development of rat pups or the germination of a seed. This cross-disciplinary drafting on the freshman level leads naturally to further cooperation between the composition staff and colleagues in other departments.

Writing in All College Courses

Faculty members in all disciplines reinforce the procedures that students have learned in composition. Professors assign extended papers in draft stages in most courses and provide most of their commentary on preliminary drafts, reserving their grades until the papers are finished. Courses in most disciplines employ a variety of collaborative learning procedures, and students must write formal acknowledgments of the responses that they receive from peers and instructors. Professors in all disciplines use writing as a mode of teaching by asking students to do brief in-class writing exercises that supplement the usual lectures and discussions. At the beginning of a class session a history instructor might ask the students to write for a few minutes on their reactions to the reading assignment. During a seminar discussion in philosophy the professor might ask all students to write down some thoughts on a challenging question. At the conclusion of a class a biology professor might ask all students to write a one-paragraph summary of the lecture. Writing has thus become an integrated part of every teaching and learning day at Beaver College.

The Writing Center

Trained undergraduate writing consultants staff the writing center, which is a place for collaborative learning, not remediation. These writing consultants are trained readers, not junior grammarians or orthographers; they help students at any stage of the writing process, from the battle against writer's block to the final proofreading. But the pencil is always in the hand of the writer, not of the consultant, and writers must formally thank the writing consultants on the acknowledgments page of the finished paper.

Writing center consultants are available during specified hours in the student activities center in a room chosen for its proximity to the student newspaper office, where students can observe how writers behave. The writing center consultants also work with students in the dormitory, sometimes during those bleak, wee hours when so many undergraduates actually confront that intimidating blank page.

The Graduate Program in the Teaching of Writing and Other Outreach Activities

Beaver College is committed to sharing its principles and practices with colleagues at all levels of education: elementary, secondary, and postsecondary. To accomplish that goal, Beaver offers a Master of Arts in English and a Master of Arts in Education with a concentration in written communications. Furthermore, during the summers of 1981 and 1982 the National Endowment for the Humanities sponsored extended institutes on the Beaver College campus for secondary and postsecondary humanists who are interested in the teaching of writing.

The Beaver College model presupposes that writing is essential to learning and that learning is a collaborative process. Our program further posits that territoriality among departments is aberrant behavior in the academy. The Beaver College program in that sense is not innovative at all. Our best hope, therefore, is that writing across the curriculum at Beaver may simply serve as a tangible reminder of what no true scholar has ever forgotten.*

Note

*This essay is reprinted from *ADE Bulletin* 69 (1981): 39–40.

Mary Oestereicher

3. Brooklyn College, City University of New York Developmental Education Program

1. **Department responsible for the writing program: Educational Services**

2. **Staffing**

Percentage of freshman composition courses taught by part-time faculty members	6%
Percentage taught by graduate students	0%
Percentage taught by full-time instructors	41%
Percentage taught by assistant, associate, and full professors	53%
Percentage taught by full-time members of departments other than English	94%

3. **Enrollment policy**

Maximum enrollment	22
Minimum enrollment	18
Average enrollment	20

4. **Program size**

   Number of students enrolled in the freshman composition program
fall 1983	180
spring 1984	160

   Number of sections of freshman composition offered
fall 1983	9
spring 1984	8

Historical Background

Students who enter college with serious deficiencies in writing skills often have cognate difficulties in reading and speech. Typically, such students are placed in separate courses to improve their performance in each area. At Brooklyn College, however, an awareness of the interdependence between writing and related language areas was the foundation for the design of a comprehensive freshman-year program. To present freshman English in a larger context, Brooklyn College's Developmental Education Program integrated writing with other communication skills and with content courses. Initially designed by a Brooklyn college Presidential Task Force, the program was established in response to a universitywide Board of Higher Education mandate to improve remedial and developmental curricula for students in SEEK (Search for Education, Elevation, and Knowledge). SEEK students are students from poverty backgrounds admitted without respect to their high school grades and assisted by supplementary funding from the state for an enriched curriculum. (The program also served as the model for a freshman program for non-SEEK students in need of intensive work.)

From its inception the Developmental Education Program was distinguished by a commitment to well-established principles of learning, such as those elucidated in the work of Benjamin Bloom, especially in his *Human Characteristics and School Learning*. Thus it was assumed that "the characteristics of the learners as well as the characteristics of the instruction can be modified in order to effect a higher level of learning" (14). Accordingly all plans for modifying cognitive behaviors were made with careful attention to the students' affective characteristics.

The aim of the Developmental Education Program was to equip freshmen with all the rhetorical skills required across the curriculum. Students were block registered in a set of courses taught by full-time instructors who met frequently in teams and who used parallel instructional units. The coordinated assignments involved narration and exposition and were tied directly to the content course work. Students' progress in each area was monitored through periodic programwide testing; the information obtained was the basis for ongoing design of instructional units. Thus the writing faculty consulted with reading and speech faculty to consider individual progress and to devise suitable strategies to meet the cognitive and affective needs of individual students. The integrated approach used in the Developmental Education Program deepened as well as broadened student understanding, yielding the outcomes most sought in freshman English programs: critical reading of a variety of texts, the ability to distinguish between objective and subjective viewpoints, clear expression and support of personal opinion, and enhanced awareness of audience.

Theoretical Assumptions

In structuring the Developmental Education Program, the faculty viewed writing and reading as the two converse processes of constructing meaning in a text. The myriad connections among these three elements—writing, reading, and text—are explored in all phases of the academic curriculum: the writing class, the reading class, the oral communication class, and the content class (called Gateway: an introduction to the social sciences or the humanities and to the liberal arts course work of the Brooklyn College core curriculum). Special emphasis is placed in all courses on the connection of writing, reading, and text to meaningfulness in the larger world. Writing and reading are regarded as purposeful activities of great use to all wishing to share in what Kenneth Bruffee, drawing on the work of Thomas Kuhn and others, envisions as the continuing conversation of the human community ("Collaborative"). Accordingly, one should hone one's skills as a writer and reader to ensure accurate communication—that is, to ensure that as a writer one may say what one means to say and that as a reader one may construe the text as it was meant to be construed. To neglect these skills is to miss the opportunity to partake more effectively of this cooperative venture, a venture that constitutes the core of liberal arts education and of a life informed by one. In the words of the program's founding director, Mervyn Keizer, the program

> reasserts the traditional responsibility of the university to give all students a solid foundation in rhetorical skills, to make them actively involved readers and writers, listeners as well as speakers, with the common theme of its reading, writing, and oral communication courses the logical development and analysis of ideas so that they may be shared. (2)

The Developmental Education Program is based on the principle that the integrated instruction of communication skills develops appreciation of varied viewpoints and the ability to argue one's own. In teaching writing, reading, and oral communication as the program's basic skills core, one teaches the universe of language. If we perceive the ultimate goals of literacy to be, on the one hand, the ability to discern relations among the ideas inherent in the messages that we receive as listeners and readers and, on the other hand, the ability to express such relations in the messages that we send as speakers and writers, then listening, speaking, reading and writing in higher education cannot be treated as wholly separate disciplines without detriment to integrated development.

To facilitate full integration, certain skills such as narrative form and library research are taught at approximately the same time by faculty members from the various disciplines. For example, students may in one month analyze narrative prose in the reading classes, write autobiographies in the writing classes, and practice the art of storytelling in the oral communication classes. Similarly, students learning to use the library may be directed to give "How to . . . " speeches on various aspects of the library for the oral communication course, while simultaneously using library resources to prepare annotated bibliographies on assigned topics for the reading classes and writing essays on the same topics for the writing classes.

Course Description

The interrelated development of writing, reading, and oral communication skills helps prepare the student for successful writing of the kind required in all college work. The long-range goal of the developmental writing course is to prepare the student to write consistently coherent expository essays in any course, on topics assigned or freely chosen. The essays should have a clear controlling purpose developed in an organized manner with supporting detail adequate for the topic and for the purpose of the essay. The writing should demonstrate the student's ability to use a variety of syntactic structures in sentence formation and a range of vocabulary sufficient to express the ideas of the essay without vagueness or redundancy. The beginnings of a personal "style" and a writer's "voice" should also be apparent. Thus the writing, in general, should be clear and natural, with no pattern of errors in regular features of standard written English and no obtrusive errors of punctuation and spelling.

To address the students' cognitive and affective needs, we use a variety of strategies in designing and sequencing writing assignments. We begin with relatively short assignments and give immediate feedback and encouragement, responding especially to the central notion expressed in the student's writing. A general model of progress is, first, to go beyond one's own experience to see other points of view; next, to see and evaluate the similarities and differences between the various points of view; and finally, to take a position informed by more than just one's own experience.

Continual writing of whole essays is required. Day-to-day instruction concentrates on the study and analysis of sentences and paragraphs. Day-to-day practice involves the production of varied, grammatically correct sentences and well-shaped, well-developed paragraphs and the combination of these paragraphs into whole essays with clear content and orderly form. The materials that the students use for study and analysis of sentence, paragraph, and essay include both samples of professionally written prose and essays written by the students themselves. The early material is chiefly narrative, the later chiefly expository.

Within the classroom, instruction consists of a variety of modes: lecture, to present and clarify new concepts; class discussion, to explore through questions and answers the initial understanding of concepts; in-class writing, to practice new concepts as well as to incorporate them into previously presented concepts; in-class guidance and supervision by instructor and tutor regarding the concepts; discussion of the students' writing in small groups with instructor and tutor overseeing and guiding the discussion; and oral presentations of written work for analysis and response by fellow students, instructor, and tutor.

Conferences and Revision Workshops

A Developmental Education Program technique that reinforces writing by drawing on reading and oral communication is the practice of conference grading. The students come to the instructor at an arranged time with a completed essay, which they read aloud. During this reading they are encouraged to amplify points orally and to consider aloud changes that could strengthen the presentation of their ideas. In this way their sense of an audience becomes vivid and concrete, as does their sense of their own voice. Further, they learn to bear in mind such an audience, albeit in the imagination, and hence become more critical readers of their own drafts. The procedure has been found to build students' confidence in themselves as thinkers and writers, as persons having worthwhile things to say—and to say in writing. As Bloom notes, "if most of the encounters with learning tasks are accompanied by appraisals of inadequacy, the individual is likely to develop a deep sense of inadequacy in connection with school acitivities" (153). The positive experience of presenting one's work to best advantage during the conference tends to replace appraisal of inadequacy with appraisal of strength. Indeed the conference may give the instructor, as well, an opportunity to gain greater confidence in the student: students with pervasive academic weaknesses often present themselves less well in a classroom setting than in a one-to-one guided conversation. Conference grading is, typically, not limited to writing teachers; the procedure is also followed effectively by content teachers.

Another common practice is holding frequent revision workshops in the classroom. Like conference grading, this technique allows for immediate feedback to both student and instructor, crucial in writing as in other disciplines:

> Unless the teacher is able to get feedback on the difficulties each student in the group has had with particular aspects of the learning task and unless each student is able to get feedback on the particular difficulties he has had with the learning task, both students and teacher must stumble on from task to task with an inadequate understanding of what learning is or is not taking place. (Bloom 28)

As one would expect, feedback very close to the time of composition seems generally to be most helpful. In the revision workshop the instructor moves around the room among a community of writers, asking questions and critiquing work in progress, aided by any tutors or peers who may read the draft. The student thus gains collaborators. The fact that everyone is writing and rewriting seems supportive, especially in encouraging weaker students to advance toward a goal that seems achievable. Final versions serve as model papers; they may be read privately, aloud, or from the blackboard. Students come to see that a variety of opinions and ways of responding to the same question are all acceptable. Again, close reading of texts and careful oral communication, as taught in related Developmental Education Program courses, maximize the effectiveness of this approach to writing.

Conclusion: Problems and Strengths

The extensive data collected and analyzed suggest both the benefits and the limitations of the Developmental Education Program approach for freshman writing (see Oestereicher). Clearly, the emphasis on individual mastery and on the interrelatedness of communication skills has aided freshmen in acquiring the writing abilities needed to pass the City University of New York Writing Assessment Test and to perform successfully in college course work. Perhaps the greatest problem has been the amount of energy and the resources needed to provide students with this kind of interdisciplinary, closely integrated instruction. Nevertheless, students and outside evaluators alike have expressed approval of the program's approach. At the end of the academic year, students have been asked their degree of satisfaction with what they accomplished in each writing area. For writing, sixty-seven percent of the students in a typical year reported that they were either very satisfied or satisfied. And in "The Developmental Education Program: A Conceptual Analysis," Kenneth Bruffee, certainly a major innovator in writing instruction, states, "In my opinion, the Developmental Education Program is among the best remedial programs I have had the opportunity to examine. It also has great promise for development into an influential model of basic skills education" (12).

Tori Haring-Smith

4. Brown University Writing Fellows Program

1. Departments responsible for the writing program: English, Dean of the College

2. Staffing

Percentage of freshman composition courses taught by part-time faculty members	0%
Percentage taught by graduate students	88%
Percentage taught by full-time instructors	0%
Percentage taught by assistant, associate, and full professors	12%
Percentage taught by full-time members of departments other than English	0%
Percentage of writing-across-the-curriculum courses taught by undergraduate tutors	100%

3. Enrollment policy

Maximum enrollment	17
Minimum enrollment	NA
Average enrollment	17+

4. Program size

Number of students enrolled in the freshman composition program

fall 1983	680
spring 1984	578

Number of sections of freshman composition offered

fall 1983	40
spring 1984	34

Students in writing-across-the-curriculum courses: 2,000 per year

---

Brown University has no writing program designed or required specifically for freshmen. Instead, Brown ensures that its students write satisfactorily by requiring writing competency for graduation. In order to determine whether a student writes competently, faculty members in all disciplines and at all levels monitor student writing. When they notice that a student's writing is not satisfactory, they indicate this deficiency in a special column provided on the final grade-report form. Students receiving two or more "deficiency checks" must improve their skills before they can graduate. In most cases, such students enroll in one or more writing courses offered by the English department. Brown has chosen this system for mandating writing competency because the ongoing attention to writing skills in all classes demonstrates to students that all faculty, and indeed all readers, value writing proficiency. Such concern is clearly not limited to the English department or to a cadre of freshman composition instructors.

Course Descriptions

Students who want to build or polish writing skills may do so through the writing curriculum administered and staffed by the English department or through the Writing Fellows Program, a writing-across-the-curriculum program funded by the dean of the college. Students with writing deficiency comprise only a small percentage of the total enrollment in the English department's writing courses. These courses in expository and creative writing attract students with a wide range of writing capabilities from all disciplines and from freshmen to seniors. The curriculum includes eight different introductory courses: basic writing (required of about 125 incoming freshmen with especially low SAT verbal scores or a poor record in high school English), scholarly and critical writing, scientific and technical writing, personal and reflective essays, and beginning courses in the writing of fiction, poetry, drama, and journalistic essays. Introductory expository writing courses are taught by graduate students who have completed at least one year of graduate work, including a course in the theory and practice of teaching writing. Introductory creative courses are taught by second-year graduate students in the creative writing program, a branch of the English department. Although the courses at this level are designed primarily for underclassmen, they also attract upperclassmen, especially those in fields where little writing is required.

Instructors in the introductory courses are given a good deal of latitude in designing their syllabi, although most subscribe to the process model, stressing the processes of invention, expression, and revision rather than the forms of discourse. No specific texts are required, and teachers must conform only to the stated course objectives. Most introductory courses include a significant reading component as well as weekly writing assignments and frequent revision.

The intermediate courses are designed for students who have mastered basic writing skills and want to extend and practice those skills. Students in these courses write well but want to know more about writing in order to gain control over their prose. In addition to courses in creative writing and journalism, this level offers an expository course in persuasive and argumentative writing that examines rhetorical techniques in advertising, law, politics, religion, and academe.

At the advanced level, designed for students who want to polish rather than build writing skills, students may take courses in creative writing, journalism, or a number of special topics that vary from semester to semester. In the past, topics like the New Journalism, travel writing, autobiography, and polemical writing have been offered. Advanced writing students also have the option of independent study credit, if they wish to work on an extended text or to study a type of writing not offered in the regular curriculum. All courses at this level are taught by the English department faculty.

Writing Fellows Program

Although extensive, this curriculum differs very little from most standard writing offerings—especially at the introductory level. It is not, however, the only writing program at Brown. In addition to a drop-in tutoring service provided by the Writing Center, the university offers its students an unusual writing-across-the-curriculum program, staffed by undergraduate peer tutors called writing fellows. While the writing curriculum serves about a thousand students a year, the writing fellows reach about two thousand. The goals of the Writing Fellows Program and the writing curriculum are complementary and not redundant. In the writing curriculum, students can focus on writing skills exclusively, while outside the English department, students can practice their writing skills as they work to understand and communicate ideas to a historian, biologist, anthropologist, or other reader with special interests and needs.

Established in the fall of 1982, the Brown University Writing Fellows Program now employs about sixty undergraduate peer tutors each year. A course participating in the Writing Fellows Program is assigned one peer tutor for every fifteen students enrolled, whether the total enrollment is fifteen or three hundred. Every paper written by every student in a participating course is first submitted to the students' writing fellow, who makes written comments on it. The papers are then returned to the students, who must revise them before submitting both versions, the original with the tutor's comments and the revision, to the faculty member in charge of the course. Although students are not required to follow the writing fellow's suggestions as they rework their papers, all students in the course must participate and must revise their work. This policy is designed to combat the students' belief that revision is a punishment meted out to poor writers rather than an integral part of any writing process. The program also demonstrates that all writing (even "passable" writing) can be improved. The policy requiring students to submit copies of both the original and the revised paper assures faculty that the peer tutor is not misleading students or acting as a ghost writer for them.

During the week or so that the students are revising their papers, they meet with their writing fellows for individual conferences. During these sessions, students may ask the writing fellows to explain their comments or to examine a draft of the students' revision. Since each student works with a particular writing fellow throughout the semester, these conferences are valuable in building a closer relationship between tutor and tutee.

Courses participating in the Writing Fellows Program vary widely from large introductory courses to small senior seminars. To be eligible for the program, a course must require students to write and revise at least two papers. The instructors of these courses are not trained to be writing instructors, nor are the course objectives altered to accommodate the writing fellows. Instead, the Writing Fellows Program works within the course without changing its structure or classroom activity. When the program started, the director had to advertise heavily the availability of writing fellows in order to interest her colleagues. Now, however, there are more faculty requests for writing fellows than the program can fulfill.

Staff Development

The writing fellows are students chosen for their proven writing ability and for their willingness to help others learn to write. Every semester, faculty members throughout the university are invited to nominate students for the Writing Fellows Program. In addition, students may nominate themselves or others. Nominees are then invited to apply for the program by submitting three samples of their prose and having a formal interview. In the summer of 1984, 160 individuals representing departments from computer science to comparative literature applied for the program's 25 open positions.

During their first semester in the program, fellows take a course in the theory and practice of the teaching of writing. In addition to examining the role of the peer tutor, this course introduces new fellows to various ways of discussing writing so that they can work effectively with students who have a variety of backgrounds and needs. Fellows practice their own writing, as well as commenting on sample student papers. Because fellows work full-time in the program while they are taking this course, they can immediately apply and test the theories they are reading.

After completing the training seminar, writing fellows continue to work in the program throughout their time at Brown. They are not required to take any further courses in the teaching of writing, but their work is supervised by the program's assistant director, an advanced graduate student with training in writing.

At the end of each semester, every fellow's work is evaluated by the assistant director and the students whom the fellow has tutored. These evaluations indicate that while students are initially fearful and defensive about showing their writing to a peer, they are converted to appreciating the program after they receive their first comments from the fellows. They realize then that the fellows are "on their side" and are helpful rather than judgmental. End-of-the-semester evaluations also indicate that over ninety percent of the students served consider the writing fellows' comments to be helpful and valid, and sixty percent report that the writing fellows helped them improve their writing skills.

Conclusion

Now in its fourth year, the program has been extremely successful. Faculty members working with it find that students' writing does improve. They are impressed not only by the quality of the writing fellows' comments but also by their students' increased awareness of writing. Students appreciate the program's ability to help them improve their writing while they are learning another subject, and they seek out courses that use writing fellows. The fellows themselves not only become highly skilled editors and teachers but also improve their own writing.

The program is successful because it responds to several needs. It increases the amount of writing that students do without increasing the number of papers that the faculty must grade, and so it allows faculty members within any discipline to emphasize writing without becoming writing teachers themselves. Whereas most writing-across-the-curriculum programs ask the faculty involved to spend a lot of time being retrained and grading papers, this program offers a service to the faculty. When faculty members participating in the program receive student papers, they can be assured that these essays were revised at least once. As a history professor noted, now he can detect and comment upon students' errors in historical methodology that used to be masked by writing problems. Furthermore, the program makes writing an active concern of the entire academic community. At Brown, writing is a subject discussed frequently in dormitories and cafeterias as well as classrooms throughout the campus. Finally, it demonstrates that some students do write well and care about helping others learn to write—not all students are like those profiled in articles on declining literacy.

The Writing Fellows Program is based upon the belief that peer tutors can provide a kind of writing instruction that is different from and in some instances preferable to instruction provided by graduate students or professors. Indeed, Brown sees the Writing Fellows Program as an ideal supplement for traditional faculty instruction. When the program was founded, it was unique in its combination of peer tutoring and writing across the curriculum. Now, however, other schools are instituting similar programs, and Brown is pleased to see that this system can work at many different kinds of institutions, from large state schools to small private colleges.

David S. Kaufer

5. Carnegie-Mellon University Freshman English Program

1. **Department responsible for the writing program: English**

2. **Staffing**

Percentage of freshman composition courses taught by part-time faculty members	5%
Percentage taught by graduate students	80%
Percentage taught by full-time instructors	0%
Percentage taught by assistant, associate, and full professors	15%
Percentage taught by full-time members of departments other than English	0%

3. **Enrollment policy**

Maximum enrollment	23
Minimum enrollment	8
Average enrollment	18

4. **Program size**

Number of students enrolled in the freshman composition program
- fall 1983   500
- spring 1984   280

Number of sections of freshman composition offered
- fall 1983   24
- spring 1984   12

Introduction

The Department of English of Carnegie-Mellon University assumes full responsibility for the freshman program and its staffing. The program is required of freshmen in every college of the university, although approximately 25–30% of the freshmen class is exempt from it. In the fall of 1983, the program mushroomed to 24 sections (an unprecedented number needed to handle the largest freshman class ever) and approximately 500 students; in the spring of 1984, it enrolled 12 sections and approximately 280 students. English graduate students seeking a professional career in writing research and pedagogy constitute approximately 80% of the staff. Another 15% consists of the director or other faculty members who serve as "mentors" to beginning teachers. The remaining 5% includes part-time faculty members who have proved themselves exceptional teachers.

The Design of the Program

The program is designed to introduce, and give students practice in, eight skills that underlie original and sustained inquiry: (1) finding problems in a text; (2) focusing a problem into a good question; (3) exploring the question for solutions; (4) turning the product (or process) of one's explorations into a linear plan for a reader; (5) turning a linear plan into a text; (6) refining a rough text into a highly polished, publishable text; (7) revising at all skill levels 1-6; (8) applying skills 1-7 recursively, to general issues addressed to general readers as well as to specialized issues and specialized readers.

To these ends, students write from two to four papers each semester and from two to four drafts of each paper. Thus they write one paper a week, though not always a finished paper. Each assignment begins with a general reading or a reading flavored by some discipline (e.g., literature, public policy, philosophy, psychology, history). Students are taught how to use the reading as a stimulus for finding their own problems to write about (skill 1 above), how to focus a problem into a good question (skill 2), and so on. Critical reading and reasoning, it should be noted, are not separated from writing.

Students attempt a draft a week and continue to write and rewrite under the teacher's supervision. It is left to the teacher's discretion to determine how much, or whether, to grade the intermediate drafts.

We hold no text sacrosanct for this course, but we do typically require either Richard E. Young, Alton L. Becker, and Kenneth L. Pike's *Rhetoric: Discovery and Change* or Linda Flower's *Problem-Solving Strategies for Writing*, since both of these books provide an intellectual basis for thinking of writing as problem solving. The only sequence of assignments we impose is from writing for general readers to writing for specialized readers. Teachers across all sections begin with reading selections that are addressed to general readers, and then we move to more disciplinary readings. This progression is designed to show students that while the problem-solving paradigm applies equally well across general and specialized discourses, writers must be sensitive to the specialized methods of defining problems and developing solutions that in some sense attend and in some sense define different academic fields.

Theoretical Assumptions

Whatever their level of skill, our students typically come to the university with radically limited, not to mention nonproductive, beliefs about writing and about their identity as writers. They come to us associating the giving of writing samples and the giving of blood. They have yet to discover the more powerful associations between academic writing and pleasure, curiosity, authority, power, dialectical inquiry, and personal growth. Resigned victims to the "writing for the teacher" syndrome, our students confuse writing with impressing the teacher or with reciting what the teacher wants to hear.

We believe we can't give students more powerful images of the writer without exposing them to the limitations of the images they already harbor. For this reason, we try, whenever possible, to apply Socratic methods in our teaching. We try to catch students in the act of doing what they normally do—and then show them why their normal strategies severely limit their power as writers. Many of our students, for example, confuse finding a problem in a reading to write about and finding the problem the author of that reading addresses. By calling our students' attention to this confusion, we can alert them to their reliance on strategies that give them no more power than the power of paraphrase.

Staffing and Teacher Training

We draw staff from our graduate programs (PhD in rhetoric, DA in English, and MA in professional writing) and handle teacher training through weekly seminar meetings and periodic visits to individual sections.

Strengths and Problems of the Program

The clear strength of the program is its energetic, committed staff members, who have a deep professional stake in writing research and pedagogy. The major problem we face arises from our success: the University, understanding that what we offer students is far from remedial English, now wants to eliminate exemptions and make advanced sections available for students who normally would be exempt. While we welcome this development in principle, it puts enormous pressures on us in practice to expand our teaching resources. A good small program can easily expand into a mediocre one. How to grow without sacrificing quality? This is the chief question we are pondering for the future.

Fredric V. Bogel

6. Cornell University Freshman Seminar Program

1. **Department responsible for the writing program: Provost**

2. **Staffing**

Percentage of freshman composition courses taught by part-time faculty members	1%
Percentage taught by graduate students	57%
Percentage taught by full-time instructors	20%
Percentage taught by assistant, associate, and full professors	22%
Percentage taught by full-time members of departments other than English	23%

3. **Enrollment policy**

Maximum enrollment	17
Minimum enrollment	NA
Average enrollment	16

4. **Program size**

   Number of students enrolled in the freshman composition program
fall 1983	3,100
spring 1984	3,000

   Number of sections of freshman composition offered
fall 1983	193
spring 1984	187

The Freshman Seminar Program (FSP) at Cornell is a yeasty mix of instruction in writing and introductory study in a wide range of disciplines. In a recent semester, the departments and programs of Africana studies, anthropology, classics, government, hotel administration, and women's studies, among many others, offered freshman seminars. The primary purpose of each seminar is to help students write competent English prose. Despite the diversity of disciplines and teaching styles represented in the program, all seminar instructors are presumed to share an energetic commitment to developing their students' ability to write.

General Principles and Theoretical Assumptions

Beyond this commitment to writing, there are probably few large notions on which all FSP staff members could be expected to agree. The practice of a sizable proportion of that staff, however, and the beliefs of the program's administrators, might be reduced to something like the following set of principles.

1. Instruction in writing is best accomplished when writing is understood generously rather than narrowly: as a complex of intellectual, rhetorical, and experiential concerns rather than as a set of "composition skills" isolated from the rest of one's education and dominated by a dread of incorrectness.
2. We, and our students, should expect writing courses to be interesting, not just necessary or instrumental. Our students should study prose because it rewards serious attention, and they should write it because we have helped them discover needs and purposes that writing answers.
3. Good writing and close reading go hand in hand. Patient, detailed attention to the texts one studies and the development of analytic and interpretive subtlety in reading foster the intellectual and verbal habits that make for effective writing. It follows that, whenever possible, a well-written text should be assigned instead of a badly written text.
4. Students profit from reading, and being asked to write in, a fairly wide range of prose forms. Insofar as the FSP has a dominant rhetorical goal, however, it is to equip students to write thoughtful argumentative and analytic essays: essays that have a point (or that take a position) and argue that point cogently.
5. Argumentative essays ought to develop an original thesis, and students should know that originality is expected of them. We cannot, of course, expect many factual discoveries (new planet, new subatomic particle), but we should expect a fresh interpretation of masterable texts and data, and we should encourage students to expect this of themselves. In practical terms, this means that, early on, students should learn to ask of their own and others' argumentative essays questions like "What's the thesis?" and "So what?" (i.e., "Is this thesis nontrivial and nonobvious?").
6. Instruction in writing should attend to the early stages of the composing process (invention, finding something to say) and the latest (serious revision). In fact, the model "invention-writing-revision" is an artificially linear sequence since our efforts to write modify our original ideas and these modifications are both revisions themselves and the source of further revisions. Invention, writing, and revision are thus strands in a rope rather than boxcars on a train.
7. Good writing depends on awareness of style. Students should be taught to look *at* prose, not just through it, and to analyze style, rhetoric, and other features of the linguistic surface. Exercises in stylistic analysis and imitation can be part of a writing course—in any field—from the beginning.
8. As much as possible, students should be encouraged to view language as a generator as well as a transmitter of meaning, "the mother, not the maid, of thought," as Karl Kraus said. Moreover, if they are taught to view the field of their seminar—sociology or

literary criticism or history—as not just a collection of facts but a perspective on the world, and a perspective that is as much linguistic as conceptual, their idea of the significance of writing will be correspondingly enlarged.
9. Students' writing improves most efficiently when individual classes and writing assignments build sequentially throughout the semester.
10. Grammar, usage, punctuation, and mechanics are most usefully taught in the context of specific writing assignments or prose analyses rather than in isolation.

Course Descriptions

In addition to study in a wide range of fields, the FSP offers a variety of approaches to the teaching of writing. Some courses focus almost entirely on writing, reading, and revision of students' essays. Some seek to integrate writing and disciplinary study; these courses treat writing as the construction of a perspective on the world and philosophy or anthropology or government as each a particular version of such perspectives (the union of a certain conceptual framework with a certain set of stylistic and rhetorical conventions). Still other courses, the majority, combine introductory readings in a particular field with detailed work on the writing of student essays. Each approach has its particular character and advantages, and it is important for the beginning TA to understand the kind of course he or she is teaching since a good deal follows from initial premises about the place of writing in a given course.

If a commitment to good student writing is the pedagogical thread presumed to unify such diversity, the following programwide guidelines serve to assure students that freshman seminars make roughly equivalent demands on them and supply roughly equivalent attention to writing.

Guidelines

1. At least thirty pages of assigned writing.
2. At least eight (and at most fourteen) written assignments.
3. Opportunities for serious revision—not mere editing—of essays. (At least some of these revising assignments may satisfy numbers 1 and 2 above.)
4. Ample classroom time (between one-half and two-thirds) spent on work that is directly related to writing.
5. Reading assignments small enough (about a hundred pages per week, at most) to permit regular, concentrated work on writing.
6. Individual conferences.

Finally, we should mention that freshman seminars are limited in enrollment to seventeen students. We hope that they will soon be smaller still (fifteen would be a reasonable maximum), but even at eighteen they are among the smallest classes that a student will take at Cornell.

Training and Support for Teaching Assistants

TAs who have not taught before, or who have some experience teaching but little or none in the teaching of writing, prepare themselves for the Freshman Seminar Program by taking either the summer or the fall version of a course in teaching writing. Those who take the summer version (Teaching Writing I) serve concurrently as apprentices in the Emphasis on Writing Program. Those who take the fall version (Teaching Writing II) teach concurrently their first course in the FSP.

The course in teaching writing combines reading in stylistics, rhetoric, and theory of composition with discussion of practical problems in the teaching of writing: correcting and grading essays; encouraging thoughtful—rather than correctly insipid—student prose; teaching stylistic analysis; teaching grammar, usage, and punctuation; using student essays in class.

In both versions of the course, though particularly in the summer, TAs work closely with experienced teachers of writing. The Freshman Seminar Program itself, moreover, provides an extension of such support in the form of course leaders: faculty members and experienced lecturers who direct multisection courses or supervise those TAs who teach single-section courses. TAs turn first to the course leader for advice on a variety of topics, especially on the particular forms that writing instruction can take in their discipline. The course leader conducts staff meetings; visits each section from time to time; advises on teaching, correcting, grading, and other tasks; and helps answer the numerous questions that afflict every beginning teacher. In addition, TAs are able to find advice, information, and support by consulting with the FSP staff and with other TAs, those struggling to stay afloat in their first writing course and those seasoned by a few semesters' teaching.

The program also supplies each instructor with a copy of *Teaching Writing: A Handbook for Instructors in the Freshman Seminar Program*. This three-hundred-page handbook includes the following chapters: "Organizing a Course," "Classroom Methods," "Understanding Prose: A Guide to the Analysis of Style," "Designing Assignments," "Correcting and Grading Essays," "Improving Sentences: Review of Grammar and Usage," and "Bibliographical Guide."

Writing Workshop

Another important resource is the Writing Workshop. The workshop performs several functions: it assesses the writing skills of many entering freshmen; it offers, in the Freshman Seminar Program, intensive tutorial workshops for students with little training in writing; it operates a walk-in service that supplies advice to students grappling with essay assignments; and it houses an experienced staff and an extensive library on writing from which the new—or experienced—teacher of writing can learn a great deal.

Lois Barry

7. Eastern Oregon State College Composition Program

1. Department responsible for the writing program: English-Writing

2. Staffing

Percentage of freshman composition courses taught by part-time faculty members	36%
Percentage taught by graduate students	0%
Percentage taught by full-time instructors	0%
Percentage taught by assistant, associate, and full professors	64%
Percentage taught by full-time members of departments other than English	0%

3. Enrollment policy

Maximum enrollment	28
Minimum enrollment	7
Average enrollment	15-25

4. Program size

Number of students enrolled in the freshman composition program

fall 1983	244
spring 1984	156

Number of sections of freshman composition offered

fall 1983	14
spring 1984	9

Historical Background

The freshman composition program at Eastern Oregon State College changed dramatically in 1975. With the encouragement of the English-Writing faculty, the college assembly voted to replace required composition courses with a writing-proficiency examination and to make all composition courses electives. This was a remarkable departure from the norm, especially for a small rural college (sixteen hundred students) in the Oregon State System of Higher Education.

For the previous ten years, EOSC had required a sequence of three-credit courses (Writing 121, 222, 323), taken during the freshman, sophomore, and junior years. (Before 1965, all three quarters of composition had been required in the freshman year.) Despite the best efforts of the English-Writing faculty, two major problems caused considerable dissatisfaction with the required composition sequence.

First, students saw writing for composition courses as separate from their "real" course work; they apparently believed that professors in other disciplines didn't care how they wrote, that only content mattered. As a result, students often interpreted composition professors' comments as nitpicking, especially when poorly written papers received high grades in other courses. Quite simply, English-Writing faculty members were more than willing to admit that they couldn't teach students to write without support from their colleagues.

Second, content professors who believed that students weren't developing adequate composition skills were assigning fewer papers. Diminished opportunities to express their ideas in writing exacerbated students' writing problems. With only 9 quarter hours out of 186 focusing specifically on composition, many students were not developing—much less refining—their abilities to write intelligent prose.

Nevertheless, after a series of meetings with the writing coordinator, content professors in each area reaffirmed their conviction that effective written expression was integral to academic success. They were willing to support the Writing Proficiency Examination (WPE) and to participate in improving their students' writing. Professors agreed that the college should guarantee each graduate's literacy; they even accepted the daunting possibility that students unable to pass the WPE would not graduate.

In 1975, the Oregon State Board of Higher Education approved EOSC's request to replace required composition courses with demonstrated writing proficiency. Perhaps the *Newsweek* article "Why Johnny Can't Write" (Sheils), published the week of their vote, influenced their decision to allow EOSC to experiment. Since that time the support of the college administration and of the state board has been consistent; in fact, board members occasionally remark that other campuses in the state system might also consider a writing-proficiency examination.

Our examination requires students to write an essay that responds to a short article in their major area. Students have three hours to write their papers. They may use dictionaries and handbooks. Essays are scored on the basis of content, organization, style, and mechanics. Volunteer readers from every discipline evaluate the essays; more than half of the teaching faculty members serve as readers. Students who fail the proficiency examination must take a writing course before taking the test again.

Course Descriptions

The move to elective composition courses allowed the English-Writing staff to make important decisions about freshman composition. Whereas we had previously required that all students take the same sequence of composition courses, we could now evaluate our students' needs and recognize that homogeneous expectations did not fit our heterogeneous student body.

Before admission, we require each student to take the SAT; we use the Test of Standard Written English (TSWE) score from the SAT for initial screening and placement in composition courses. To verify placement decisions, students write an in-class diagnostic essay during the first week of the term. A few students are moved to other levels of composition, but the TSWE scores provide correct placement for more than ninety percent of incoming freshmen.

Following the profile of students' basic writing skills provided by TSWE data, we added two composition courses for freshmen whose test scores indicated verbal deficiencies. Writing 040, a non-graduation-credit course, focuses on sentence-level skills (for students with a TSWE score below 30). Small class size (15) also provides a supportive environment for students with writing anxieties. Writing 115 (TSWE 30-36) is an introduction to expository writing (enrollment 18) designed to develop fluency and paragraph skills. Freshmen advisers consult with students about their entry scores, pointing out writing courses at the appropriate level, but the choice remains with the student. No student is required to take a specific writing course. This reserves valuable staff time for instructing those students who are sufficiently motivated to benefit from reviewing the essentials of composition. We no longer require uninterested students to occupy chairs in fall-term composition courses simply because their last names begin with A-J.

Until 1975, all freshmen were placed in Writing 121, often with discouraging results. By offering these new courses, we hope to temper the revolving-door aspect of our virtually open-door enrollment. Because we require all students to demonstrate writing proficiency before graduation, we also have assumed an ethical obligation to teach motivated students to write. For this reason, unlike most other colleges in the Oregon system, we do not charge extra fees for Writing 040, a developmental course. Our records indicate that the revised curriculum has benefited students who would otherwise have dropped out of school. Students entering with verbal scores below 30 have successfully worked their way through a series of writing courses—from Writing 040 to Writing 115 to Writing 121 to one or more Writing 225s—and graduated, having passed the Writing Proficiency Examination.

After the writing coordinator participated in the first University of Iowa Institute on Writing in 1979, a further modification of the freshman composition program occurred. The standard freshman composition course, Writing 121 (Expository Writing, 3 credits), was separated into two five-credit courses: Expository Writing Workshop and Exploratory Writing Workshop, each meeting five days a week.

The Expository Workshop remains fairly traditional. Each professor selects a text for the course, usually one organized by the modes of discourse. Most teachers emphasize organization, revising imprecise passages, and correcting errors. Specific instruction is provided on organizational patterns, stylistic choices, and error avoidance. Anthologized essays often serve as the springboard for students' themes. The instructor is the primary audience for student writing; every paper is graded. Depending on the professor, between five and ten papers are required during the quarter. Most are revised to incorporate the instructor's comments and corrections.

The Exploratory Workshop encourages faculty to incorporate as much of the new composition theory as they wish. National and regional conferences, the Iowa Institute on Writing, the National Writing Project, and National Council of Teachers of English and Boynton/Cook publications all have influenced the Exploratory Writing pedagogy. In the Exploratory Workshop, a sequence of approximately twenty assignments leads students to develop enthusiasm for writing as well as refining their composing skills. During the first two weeks of the quarter, students write short fail-safe papers. These early daily assignments are as different from traditional 500-word themes as the imaginations of the instructors will allow—for instance, grappling with a perceptual problem and writing about puzzle-solving attitudes, writing paragraphs using only words of one syllable and writing in-class responses to unusual objects provided by the instructor.

In Exploratory Writing, peer-response groups clarify the distinction between writer-based and reader-based prose. Professors encourage a congenial workshop atmosphere with positive responses to the best passages of students' papers, followed by questions and requests for additional information. Since students are writing from their own observations, experiences, and perceptions, they are experts on the topics they write about; they must therefore accept responsibility for expanding on or clarifying problematic passages. Throughout the term, duplicated student papers comprise the text for the course. Papers, all considered works in progress, are not graded. Appropriate stylistic choices and revision techniques are discussed as specific issues appear in duplicated papers. Students are expected to generate between 7,500 and 10,000 words in a quarter and to revise and submit about 2,500 words for a final grade. An outline of Exploratory Writing course objectives follows:

1. to familiarize students through practice with the stages of the writing process—prewriting, composing, revising, and editing;
2. to develop students' syntactic fluency through frequent writing experiences, both graded and ungraded;
3. to introduce students to strategies and heuristics that will help them to discover a topic;
4. to acquaint students with the benefits of writing multiple drafts of a paper, incorporating suggestions for development, and applying revision techniques introduced during the term;
5. to prepare students to support general statements with specific details, frequently drawing upon personal experience to develop their topics;
6. to acquaint students with the importance of an honest, consistent voice as a basis for effective communication;
7. to alert students to the importance of both global and local revision of their writing, ranging from overall organizational patterns to specific word choice;
8. to acquaint students with stylistic choices appropriate to writing for different audiences and different purposes;
9. to encourage students to use figurative language when appropriate;
10. to inform students that skills in clear written expression transfer to any writing situation.

Students choose between the freshman course options according to their expectations and experience. Those freshmen who feel insecure about academic writing tend to choose Expository Writing. Many of these students, educated in small rural high schools, believe they have missed essential writing instruction; they are looking for a back-to-the-basics course. They welcome relatively formulaic approaches to expressing their ideas and respond favorably to the more traditional orientation of Expository Writing. On the other hand, students who disliked their traditional high school composition courses select the student-centered course, Exploratory Writing. Their choices may be informed not so much by what they *do* want as by previous negative experiences they are determined to avoid repeating. Having completed either Expository Writing or Exploratory Writing, students may also take the other for credit.

Even though the process-oriented theorists seem to dominate the scholarly journals, the product-oriented textbook publishers proceed unabashed. Our freshman composition options reflect these two worlds; both faculty members and students seem content with their choices. Expository and exploratory sections are offered each term. Because every student must pass the Writing Proficiency Examination before graduation, we are naturally concerned that both courses develop essential writing competencies. Expository Writing develops those writing skills deductively, whereas Exploratory Writing achieves the same objectives inductively.

Staffing and Teacher Training

Because EOSC is a four-year college, offering graduate degrees only in education, freshman composition is taught almost exclusively by seven full-time English-Writing faculty members, who are also responsible for teaching journalism, imaginative writing, and language arts methods for teacher education. Two part-time adjunct staff members currently teach sections of Writing 115. These instructors work informally with the writing coordinator; because they have had recent experience with student-centered composition theory, their training has not been a problem. We have no graduate assistants.

As is typical of most college English faculties, our professors were educated in the belletristic tradition. Those who have demonstrated a commitment to teaching composition are largely self-taught. Staff attitudes toward teaching composition range from dutiful to enthusiastic. With one exception, all full-time English-Writing faculty members teach both composition and literature courses. This shared obligation is important to maintaining collegiality and encouraging dialogue.

Just as writing is a highly individual enterprise, so is teaching writing. It seems inappropriate, if not impossible, to mandate a single philosophy or pedagogy to an experienced staff, most with over fifteen years' teaching experience. The option of teaching either of the parallel freshman courses (Expository Writing or Exploratory Writing) allows faculty members to choose an approach consistent with their training and inclinations. There is no doubt that professors who choose to teach Exploratory Writing find the nontraditional format engaging; they welcome the challenge of crafting effective assignments and enjoy the vitality of students' papers. They are also pleased by students' positive responses to a "different" freshman composition course.

Strengths and Problems of the Program

When the shift from required to elective composition was made, all staff noticed a marked improvement in students' attitudes toward writing classes. Understandably, student reaction to the Writing Proficiency Examination as a graduation requirement was not nearly so positive. Initially, students threatened to transfer to other colleges to avoid the WPE, but no decrease in enrollment resulted; if EOSC lost students, they were replaced by others. The WPE has been in place for nine years, and students no longer exert much energy attempting to eliminate it. This requirement, unlike the previous freshman composition requirement, addresses the needs of students dedicated to completing a four-year program. These students are committed to learning a skill they must master in order to graduate.

The writing-across-the-curriculum program that accompanied the initiation of the Writing Proficiency Examination was designed primarily to help professors appreciate how writing could enhance students' learning in content courses. Realizing that continual writing practice would make students increasingly proficient, we believed that writing for learning would complement the writing courses that students chose to take. Unfortunately, there has been a recent shift in some faculty members' attitudes about responsibility for developing students' writing skills; the focus once again seems to be turning to composition courses. A considerable turnover in teaching faculty may explain this recidivism. At orientation, new faculty members are introduced to the Writing Proficiency Examination and are provided with a handbook written by the writing coordinator, "The Busy Professor's Travel Guide to Writing across the Curriculum." However, recently appointed faculty have not participated in the summer writing-across-the-curriculum workshops that were held from 1979 to 1983. There is a marked difference between knowing about writing across the curriculum and knowing that it is essential to develop students' learning and to maintain their writing skills. Another series of meetings with professors from various disciplines may be necessary to correct misconceptions and to generate understanding of EOSC's commitment to sharing responsibility for improving students' writing.

On the other hand, a number of faculty members in various disciplines regularly assign both in-class and out-of-class writing to enhance understanding of course concepts. Current discussions with these professors aim at creating split-prefix courses, for instance, Soc-Wr, Phil-Wr, or Bio-Wr. These upper-division courses will incorporate a significant variety of writing assignments (not just term papers) in their syllabi. Professors will respond to writing style as well as to content and will be encouraged to provide opportunities for peer responses to initial drafts.

An additional problem has resulted from the trade-offs necessary when the five-credit freshman composition courses were created. The other two courses, previously three credits, were reduced to two credits. Although the junior-level course, Advanced Exposition (Writing 316), has recently become five credits, the sophomore-level courses remain two credits. Faculty members are frustrated by the limited instructional time. They hope to see Writing 225, Intermediate Prose, eventually become a five-credit course as well. At the moment, staffing limitations make that shift unlikely. The same limitations occasionally raise course enrollments above the designated maximums, creating less than ideal circumstances for both students and professors.

Overall, the benefits of curricular changes have certainly outweighed the disadvantages. In a time of diminished regard for standards in higher education, the notation on each graduate's transcript, "Writing Proficiency Examination Passed," has been a positive factor in the placement of EOSC graduates, especially for education majors.

Those freshmen whose writing skills are far above average have gained flexibility in their schedules by passing the Writing Proficiency Examination after only one writing course. The needs of a larger number of students, those who require more than nine hours of composition, are being met by Writing 040 and Writing 115. The writing faculty appreciates that students in Writing 121 and Writing 131 are reasonably well prepared for college-level composition. The change from required to elective courses and the options of expository or exploratory approaches to freshman composition have allowed both students and faculty to attain a gratifyingly compatible learning/teaching environment.

Marie Wilson Nelson

8. George Mason University Required Writing Program

1. **Department responsible for the writing program: English**

2. **Staffing**

Percentage of courses taught by part-time faculty members	45%
Percentage taught by graduate students	45%
Percentage taught by full-time instructors	0%
Percentage taught by assistant, associate, and full professors	10%
Percentage taught by full-time members of departments other than English	0%

3. **Enrollment policy**

Maximum enrollment	27
Minimum enrollment	9
Average enrollment	27

4. **Program size**

    Number of students enrolled in the program
fall 1983	1,875
spring 1984	847

    Number of sections of offered
fall 1983	73
spring 1984	46

The required writing program at George Mason University includes three components: required courses and their alternatives; two supplementary writing support centers; and a training program for graduate students who teach in the undergraduate program (English 101 and 102 and the two tutorial centers). The three components reflect a common philosophy rooted in three beliefs: (1) that personal knowledge, experience, and curiosity motivate writing growth; (2) that learning to write involves learning strategies for generating ideas, for getting them down on paper, for revising drafts, for editing and formatting for appropriate audiences, and for making constructive use of responses at all stages in the development of a piece; and (3) that writing leads to discoveries about what one knows or is trying to learn.

Program Outline

Required Courses and Alternatives

English 101—a three-credit writing course in which students participate in such activities as writing daily; responding to one another's writing in small groups; revising, editing, and publishing their better pieces; discussing writing problems and successful strategies; and using writing as a tool for understanding material from other courses. Some sections of this course are taught by graduate students trained at GMU.

English 100—a four-credit alternative to English 101 with enrollment limited to nonnative speakers of English. This course is taught by faculty members with expertise in teaching English as a Second Language.

English 102—our traditional second course on writing in response to literature. Sections are taught by faculty members or by experienced graduate teaching assistants. (For students in most majors, this course is now being replaced by English 302.)

English 302—an array of three preprofessional writing courses (for social science, natural science, and liberal arts students respectively), one of which is taken as students begin work in their major fields. The goal of these courses is to provide practice with the kinds of writing done in various areas of specialization and to extend writing instruction across the student's college career. All sections are taught by faculty members.

The writing-across-the-curriculum component of PAGE (Plan for Alternative General Education)—writing instruction built into the interdisciplinary courses of this general education program by means of continuing faculty development in the teaching of writing. Taught by faculty members from many disciplines, writing across the curriculum in PAGE replaces the separate writing courses described above. A writing specialist receives one course of released time per semester to help faculty members teach writing in the context of individual courses.

The Writing Centers

GMU's two writing centers address student writing problems in similar but complementary ways. Both are administered by faculty members and staffed by graduate teaching assistants who, like TAs in English 101 and 102, participate in a two-week workshop before their teaching assignments begin and complete a three-credit seminar in the teaching of writing during their first semester of tutoring.

The Writing Place, established by the English department, offers one-to-one or small-group tutorial help on course assignments and other specific writing tasks, by appointment, to university students, faculty, and staff. Writing Place tutors help with a variety of problems, from overcoming blocks to formulating ideas, revising, organizing, and editing drafts. The Writing Place is funded for fifty instructional hours a week and serves approximately 500 students a year; 39% of these are ESL students. Average attendance is three sessions per client. Students needing systematic help may be referred to the Composition Tutorial Center.

The Composition Tutorial Center (CTC), established by GMU's faculty senate to help entering students with identified writing problems, provides two noncredit, hour-long writing workshops a week. Four or five basic writers meet with the same tutor for a semester or until earning certification. As with the Writing Place, the goal is developing confidence and independence with all phases of writing. In contrast to the Writing Place, CTC students do not work with course assignments made by other teachers. Initially conceived as a remedial center, the CTC provides groups for 350 to 400 writers a year, 40% of whom are nonnative speakers of English. Volunteers and already certified writers who are willing to attend regularly also participate on a space-available basis.

The Training Program for Graduate Teaching Assistants

Graduate students are selected on a competitive basis from applicants in all disciplines. To date, most applications have come from our MA or MFA programs in poetry, fiction, and professional writing and editing or in linguistics, literature, or the teaching of writing and literature. Preference is given to experienced writers and/or second-language users whose ideas about teaching basic and ESL writers are rooted in awareness of what helps their own writing improve.

All TAs attend an intensive two-week workshop offered the last two weeks in August to prepare them for the first weeks of school. Two three-hour limited-enrollment courses in teaching writing are also offered during fall semester, one required of TAs for English 101 and 102, the other of tutors in the tutorial centers. These include such activities as studying research and theory in writing and language acquisition; practicing self-selected writing and writing-to-learn strategies to experience what they will be preparing students to do; working in small, supportive groups to experience the effects of such groups; examining their writing practices and how they learned to write; evaluating methods in the light of their combined experience as writers; observing experienced teachers demonstrate successful methods; talking to former TAs who have been particularly successful; and keeping teacher-research logs (or audio- or videotaping) in order to record and reflect on what works in their own teaching.

Basic Assumptions

The following assumptions underlie all three components of George Mason's program and have shaped its evolution:

1. Writing is natural.
2. Everyone can learn to write well.
3. Learning to write is developmental and requires practice over time.
4. We learn to write by writing for our own purposes.

5. We pick up writing strategies and formal techniques from other writers.
6. We learn from our mistakes.
7. Writing is a way of learning and of identifying tacit knowledge.
8. Anxiety interferes with learning.
9. ESL writers, dialect writers, and standard English writers are fundamentally similar in the way they write and learn to write.
10. Writing abilities develop naturally when writers control language choices.
11. Personal writing experience is a valid guide for teaching.

The operation of the small-group Composition Tutorial Center and of writing across the curriculum in PAGE will illustrate how these assumptions shape practice throughout George Mason's required writing program.

The Composition Tutorial Center

CTC tutoring reflects several conscious emphases: reproducing conditions under which real-world writing takes place, maintaining a safe atmosphere in which writers are not penalized for experimenting (even when their experiments fail), letting group activities grow naturally from what writing students choose, fostering independence and responsibility, and generalizing newly learned writing strategies to academic and nonacademic writing. Each of these emphases is in turn reflected in specific actions:

1. Tutors replicate conditions of nonschool writing communities by:

   - having students write every day;
   - relying on intrinsic rewards—satisfaction, pride, pleasure, catharsis, self-understanding, feelings of accomplishment, and so on—rather than on grades to motivate student writers;
   - providing expanding audiences for writers (heterogeneous groups for sharing, the weekly *CTC Excerpts,* four bulletin boards for displaying the best of student writing, publication of a CTC book at the end of each semester);
   - responding as fellow writers rather than tutors or teachers;
   - modeling attitudes typical of writers;
   - demonstrating behaviors tutors themselves use when they write;
   - demonstrating the kinds of writing responses they themselves prefer;
   - helping students separate and sequence writing tasks;
   - separating learning to write from learning subject-area content;
   - cycling students repeatedly through all phases of writing—from the search for topics to drafting, revising, editing, and publication;
   - shifting the focus gradually from deep structure to surface structure (from content to organization to editing) during the development of individual papers and across the course of a term;
   - sharing, displaying, and publishing papers at various stages of completion;
   - encouraging collaborative solutions to writing problems;

- avoiding teaching approaches tutors themselves find unhelpful.

2. Tutors maintain a safe atmosphere by

- rewarding experiments rather than penalizing those that fail;
- abolishing grades (except for the mandated certification process);
- functioning as advocates, not as evaluators;
- identifying strengths before making suggestions for improvement;
- limiting criticism to a few constructive suggestions per draft;
- letting most suggestions for improvement come from students;
- removing from the groups students who cut down others or others' work.

3. Tutors let group activities grow naturally from what the writing students choose to do by

- having students read their work aloud regularly to develop a sense of how others perceive it;
- pointing out strengths in every piece of writing;
- suggesting alternatives to rigid rules and error-avoidance strategies;
- drawing on personal and group experience for writing advice;
- modeling the search for answers when the tutor or group is stumped;
- teaching incidentally, as problems arise in student writing, regardless of the type of help required (invention strategies, organization, transitions, grammatical and mechanical rules, diction, style, etc.);
- teaching rules one at a time and at the point of need.

4. Tutors encourage independence and responsibility by

- having students choose their own topics, genres, and audiences;
- letting the groups decide what works or fails in a piece;
- having writers keep process logs and use "thinkwriting" strategies to solve their own writing problems, to evaluate their own progress and to decide what they need to work on next;
- teaching intuitive monitoring strategies;
- teaching students to engage and disengage the monitor as needed at varying stages in the process;
- letting the writers determine how much revising to do;
- eliminating required homework;
- placing responsibility for group effectiveness on students;
- withdrawing gradually from tutoring roles to serve as resource people.

5. Tutors help students generalize newly learned writing strategies to academic and other writing tasks by

- brainstorming ways to apply writing strategies picked up in the center to assignments for other courses;
- letting students ask one another for suggestions when they have trou-

ble with papers for other courses or with out-of-school writing tasks (instead of letting them work on such papers directly in the center);
- teaching students to reorganize and provide missing transitions, thesis statements, and so on to a written draft;
- encouraging students to talk about out-of-school writing they do;
- teaching students "thinkwriting" strategies for use in other courses.

Several characteristics of the CTC approach are noteworthy. In the first place, the five-student groups have proven cost-effective and unexpectedly successful with basic and ESL writers. A few tutors are able to help large numbers of students; in fact, our experience scheduling groups of various sizes shows that those in groups of four or five become independent writers more quickly than do students tutored individually or in groups of two or three. This seems to happen because the larger groups generate more student suggestions for improvement. As a result, writers begin to rely on one another and begin to trust their ability to make decisions without the tutor. Also, because group interactions develop naturally from the strengths and weaknesses of pieces drafted and read in group, tutors need little preparation time and can spend all working hours with students in groups.

Second, we find that heterogeneous groups learn faster, and we now deliberately schedule groups to maximize differences. The middle-aged suburban woman with the GED certificate and the recent Korean immigrant with a 770 score on the math section of the SAT learn more from each other than they do when grouped by "ability" or language background. Minority and language-minority students, eighteen- and fifty-year-olds, learn to trust and help each other make their writing better. ESL and native English writers become partners, the native speakers giving ESL students no more than they receive in return.

Third, the CTC's collaborative atmosphere provides for a sufficiency of success, with students themselves determining when their efforts fall short. As they help each other, competing only against themselves, writing anxiety decreases, as do other affective barriers to learning. Students who enter the center resistant and defensive show increasing involvement and determination to write well. In the safety of the CTC, where writers' freedom is protected and mutual support required, basic and ESL students experience the rewards of academic groups, the benefits of joining a writing community, the pleasures of being what Frank Smith calls "members of the club." When this happens, we see changes in attitude and diligence, both of which lead, in time, to improved written work.

Writing across the Curriculum in PAGE

George Mason's new Plan for Alternative General Education (PAGE) offers freshmen and sophomores the option of interdisciplinary learning. Developed under state grants for faculty and program development, the PAGE curriculum fulfills science, humanities, English, mathematics, social science, and non-Western culture requirements. By bringing together faculty from many fields for course development and team teaching, PAGE provides a coherence rarely achieved in general education, particularly in a seventeen-thousand-student state university.

PAGE pursues and extends the aims of the "writing to learn" movement, many of which also shape the required courses described above, by having students use writing, speaking, problem solving, and computers in every course. In all the disciplines they encounter, students get writing practice and guidance in using appropriate strategies and forms. In four semesters of such courses as Reading the Arts, Quantitative Analysis, and Technology and Society, PAGE students write lab reports, computer programs, autobiography, a variety of analytical essays, and research reports based on personal curiosity, surveys, interviews, and library study. In learning logs they record impressionistic and analytical responses to readings, brainstorm solutions to practical problems, and explore connections between new information and old. The widespread use of learning logs, particularly in the first year, helps writers discover connections among their different courses and provides direct and indirect feedback on our teaching effectiveness. In short, because this program and its individual courses are conceived and administered in an interdisciplinary way, we ensure that all students practice writing for diverse audiences and purposes.

In PAGE, through large- and small-group work, problem solving is integrated with writing and speaking to learn. A rule of thumb we follow in designing courses, for example, is that writing assignments must be integral to the learning goals of each course. As a result, student writing is used less often as a test of knowledge than as a vehicle for elaborating and refining thought, as a means of discovering complexity, of examining relations among ideas. Since thinking is in many ways a collaborative process, we provide opportunities for both teacher and peer response during the development of written and oral projects. Several of the twelve courses use writing-discussion-speaking workshops to help students design, research, write up, and present individual or group projects. The goals are increased fluency with academic language and the growth of collaborative decision-making abilities students will need after graduation.

Writing across the curriculum in PAGE is achieved through faculty training coordinated by a writing-across-the-curriculum specialist. We are also fortunate that another writing specialist serves as director of PAGE. In addition, several faculty members have participated in intensive faculty writing projects conducted during the past few years by GMU's Northern Virginia Writing Project. Since faculty members work in teams to develop and refine courses and work in pairs to teach individual sections of a course, those knowledgeable about writing can help others broaden their understanding of the uses of writing in teaching. The teams also provide a forum in which the writing specialist can answer questions, provide support for experimentation, and present new techniques.

At George Mason University we assume we will get students with varied language skills and that their writing will develop naturally under the right conditions. We therefore try to provide conditions conducive to writing and a variety of writing options from which students may choose. We believe writing is much more than a way of documenting verbal or academic skills. In addition to its function as a channel for communication, we value it also as a means of self-expression, of creating and re-creating experience, of delighting others and ourselves; we use it as a tool for learning, a way of integrating new knowledge with old, a heuristic for personal and academic problem solving, a help in understanding ourselves and our world.

James F. Slevin

9. Georgetown University Composition Program

1. Department responsible for the writing program: English

2. Staffing

Percentage of freshman composition courses taught by part-time faculty members	0%
Percentage taught by graduate students	0%
Percentage taught by full-time instructors	0%
Percentage taught by assistant, associate, and full professors	100%
Percentage taught by full-time members of departments other than English	0%

3. Enrollment policy

Maximum enrollment	15
Minimum enrollment	12
Average enrollment	14

4. Program size

Number of students enrolled in the freshman composition program
fall 1983	155
spring 1984	35

Number of sections of freshman composition offered
fall 1983	11
spring 1984	3

The Georgetown University Composition Program encompasses a small but crucial part of our English department's course offerings. I will not focus here on our intermediate, advanced, or graduate writing courses, because these probably differ only slightly from such courses at other universities. Nor will I focus on the majority of our introductory English classes, called Literature and Writing; these courses combine the study of literature with extensive work on student writing. I will concentrate instead on those of our freshman composition offerings that seem distinctive. After discussing two special writing programs (the Liberal Studies Program and the Expository Writing Program), I will return to a consideration of how we are starting to connect literature and writing, interpretation and composition, in all our courses.

The Liberal Studies Program

The Liberal Studies Program for Community Scholars is a sequence of courses, centered in the English department, which provides approximately forty-five minority students each year with an intensive introduction to effective academic writing. Coordinated by Paul Cardaci, this program brings together students whose academic backgrounds might impair their success in our regular freshman courses. For three weeks during the summer, Georgetown offers three sections of an intensive writing course, with fifteen students per section. These students not only receive the individualized attention of the professor but are also provided with tutorial help from graduate and undergraduate tutors. Each English teacher organizes his or her course as a workshop that focuses on précis writing and the critical analysis of expository and persuasive prose. To supplement the work of the course, tutors meet regularly with students in small groups and also provide individual instruction for up to two hours per week. The goal of this summer program is to introduce the students to basic principles of organization and higher-order reasoning. By the end of the summer, the students are better prepared for the types of courses they will be taking in the fall semester.

Most of their course work in the fall semester is structured around their freshman English course. All students are enrolled in a philosophy course and a history of Western civilization course, both of which are carefully coordinated with their English course. The English instructor attends the lectures of the other two courses and meets regularly with the professors of these courses to discuss paper topics and other requirements. The students are assisted in all their courses (English, philosophy, history) by tutors who are pursuing advanced degrees in these disciplines, and these tutors also meet regularly with the English professor to receive guidance. The English course can therefore be devoted to basic principles of academic writing, not in some abstract manner but in direct and specific relation to the essays being prepared for the two other courses.

In the spring semester, most of the students enter Georgetown's regular program of studies, taking a freshman literature and writing course and three or four of the university's general education requirements (which include another semester of history, theology, science, etc.). For those students whose writing still demands special, concentrated attention, the spring semester replicates the fall semester, only now the English composition course is coordinated with a history and a theology course. By the end of the spring semester, nearly all the students are ready to enroll in our regular curriculum. Those few who still require special help are served by the normal resources of the university: our freshman literature and writing course supplemented by individualized tutoring in the university's Writing Center.

The Expository Writing Program and Its Staffing

In addition to the three composition courses within the Liberal Studies Program, Georgetown offers each fall semester anywhere from eight to ten sections of expository writing. At the beginning of the semester, entering freshmen take a placement examination (a writing sample evaluated by the English department faculty). Those who can benefit most from the concentrated study of composition are enrolled in one of these expository writing sections. Our program is unique not only in the content and goals of these courses but also in our manner of staffing them.

Georgetown's English faculty is not unique in its academic background. Nearly all members of the department received their PhDs in some area of literary study, and while we work closely with student writing in all our courses (freshman, upper-division, and graduate), we have not, by and large, been trained to teach writing—at least not by the standards of current research in rhetorical theory. To take advantage of our genuine desire to teach composition and to remedy our flawed graduate preparation, the department has established a program that, with the advice and assistance of some of our best graduate students, in effect retrains our literature faculty.

Thanks in part to a grant from the National Endowment for the Humanities, each year Georgetown awards full fellowships to four experienced high school teachers who wish to pursue a master's degree that combines the study of literature with the study of composition. They enter a program in which they study both literature and literary theory and current research on rhetoric and composition pedagogy. Each of these graduate student-teachers, known as Writing Center associates, is paired with a Georgetown professor who has not regularly taught a section of expository writing, and together they team-teach two sections of this course. They plan and conduct classroom activities, share the paper load, hold individual conferences with students, and so on. In addition to this direct attention from their teachers, students enrolled in these writing classes receive special help (between one and two hours per week) from undergraduate tutors in the University Writing Center. The Georgetown faculty member and the graduate student-teacher meet regularly with the tutors to guide their work and listen to suggestions about student needs.

Our Writing Center associates are thus in direct contact with more students, for more hours, than any other graduate teaching fellows at Georgetown. They do our students an extraordinary service, while gaining from the experience a clearer sense of how their own teaching can better prepare their high school students for postsecondary education. They also do wonders for the Georgetown teachers with whom they work. We have come to value them as colleagues who, because of their talent and experience, can often do a better job with our freshmen than we can and who certainly have a great deal to contribute to our own development, especially as teachers of writing.

Each teaching team conducts its course as it thinks best; that is, Georgetown has no preestablished composition syllabus. As coordinator of this program, I meet weekly with the eight teachers to discuss theoretical articles relevant to the teaching of writing, exploring the application of current literary and composition theory to pedagogy. These staff meetings engage fundamental questions about the goals of writing courses and, more generally, of English studies. We explore the relationships between interpreting and composing discourse, looking for connections based on contemporary theories of textuality. We examine the function of figurative language in both literary and nonliterary forms of discourse, and we have even begun to call into question distinctions between literary and nonliterary genres and styles. The discussions, then, focus on issues that have as much relevance to the teaching of literature as to the teaching of composition, and the tentative conclusions we have been able to draw have already influenced curriculum and pedagogy throughout our English department offerings.

After participating in the program, many faculty members have significantly altered their conceptions of literary study, concentrating far more than they did before on the place of writing in what they do as teachers of English. These changes are of course as much indebted to developments in current literary theory as they are to the insights of composition research. Rhetorical critics like Kenneth Burke and Wayne Booth, reader-response theorists like Stanley Fish and Wolfgang Iser, anthropological critics like Clifford Geertz and Walter Ong, semioticians like Robert Scholes, and deconstructionists like J. Hillis Miller have had as much influence on our program as have the established figures in composition theory. As a result, the boundaries between our composition courses and our literature courses have begun to dissolve, and former participants in the program report that they are now teaching their literature courses as writing courses, with *writing* understood both as a content (the texts of the courses are "writing" as we now understand the term) and as a process through which students can come to understand those texts and even produce them. This new way of understanding textuality is leading us gradually to a reintegration of the English curriculum, a convergence that brings coherence not only to our courses but to our sense of our own collegiality.

Mathilda Liberman

10. Grinnell College Writing Program

1. **Department responsible for the writing program: Dean of the Faculty**

2. **Staffing**

Percentage of freshman composition courses taught by part-time faculty members	0%
Percentage taught by graduate students	0%
Percentage taught by full-time instructors	10%
Percentage taught by assistant, associate, and full professors	90%
Percentage taught by full-time members of departments other than English	90%

3. **Enrollment policy**

Maximum enrollment	13
Minimum enrollment	NA
Average enrollment	13

4. **Program size**

   Number of students enrolled in the freshman composition program
fall 1983	344
fall 1984	389

   Number of sections of freshman composition offered
fall 1983	25
fall 1984	30

Grinnell College employs a cross-disciplinary approach to the teaching of composition, in a complex program administered by the dean of the faculty and her associates. There is no composition course as such. There is, however, the freshman tutorial, which in some respects substitutes for a composition course. The tutorials, no matter how many are required, and all other courses with a composition emphasis are taught by regular faculty without respect to rank. Only College Writing 104, a basic composition course offered to a small number of students each semester, is taught by Writing Lab instructors, who are not included within the regular faculty.

Grinnell adopted the freshman tutorial in 1972, when collegewide requirements were abolished in favor of an elective program. The tutorial is the only required course: all freshmen must take it in their first semester. There are, to be sure, other constraints on the students' academic choices:

each department enforces its own set of prerequisites for the major, and the advisers, who have considerable influence, steer their charges toward a program that satisfies not only the students' individual interests but also the general standards of a liberal education. In other words, Grinnell College students are expected to take courses in three divisions (humanities, science, and social studies) and to acquire the skills that make knowledge in the selected disciplines possible and effective. In the latter category, the college emphasizes foreign languages, writing, computer literacy, and the quantitative studies that underlie the methods of the various social and natural sciences.

Freshman Tutorials

The freshman tutorials play an important part in this scheme. These groups meet in an informal setting and are taught by professors selected each year from various departments. These tutors function in several ways: they are academic advisers to the students in the groups, helping each of them to plan the freshman and sophomore years (after which the major adviser takes over), and they design their own tutorials, generally selecting a topic related in some fashion to their disciplines and structured to emphasize methods of inquiry and research techniques rather than the mastery of disciplinary material. The titles of a few tutorials indicate some typical approaches to subject matter: Intimations of God in Contemporary Fiction (taught by a professor of philosophy), Current Issues of Biomedical Ethics (chemistry), Technology, Corporate Capitalism, and American Values (anthropology), and American Musical Theatre (music).

Last but not least, tutors must offer practice in writing, oral presentation, and the analysis of texts. Thus they are the students' first rhetoric teachers, assigning papers (to speak only of written work) that include such forms as the one-page note on some aspect of a text or problem, the more ambitious critical analysis and argument, and, in the final weeks, the research paper that requires a synthesis of the topic or some aspect of it.

The rationale for such a course, in which composition is taught by professors from all departments (in 1984 only four tutorials were designed by English professors), is that the entire college, not just one of its departments, is responsible for promoting high standards of literacy in the students. Most professors use writing not only to promote learning but also to test their students' mastery of the material; to this end they assign papers—and grade and criticize them—on the basis of criteria relevant to their disciplines. In light of this practice, it makes no sense, in a liberal arts college, to hold the English department (which has its own disciplinary aims) solely responsible for teaching the modes and ends of written discourse.

The tutorial is, thus, simply the first point at which the Grinnell student is introduced to the college's demands for literate discourse. Apart from the usual emphasis on writing throughout the curriculum, the college each semester designates certain sections of regularly scheduled courses as writing-intensive. In these courses, special emphasis is given to expository writing in the context, again, of a specific subject matter. Five papers of increasing complexity are assigned, and enrollment is limited to twenty students to allow the instructor time for attending to their individual writing needs. All sections of

Humanities 101 (The Greek World), several sections of English 107 (Literary Problems), and, when possible, single sections of standard courses in such disciplines as economics, anthropology, sociology, philosophy, and history are so designated each semester.

Faculty Development

The college's commitment to writing across the curriculum has required it to invest in faculty development. In 1974, with the help of the English department, the college introduced the faculty writing seminars, which, under the direction of the dean and the director of the Writing Lab, continue to this day. These seminars consist of six or seven participants and a leader, all from different departments, who, for a stipend (the leader is paid more than the participants), meet for a week in the summer to go over student papers they themselves have assigned and graded. During this time they review the conventions of English grammar and usage and other principles of good composition and in the process try to develop a common approach to the use and evaluation of student writing.

The first of these seminars, as can be imagined, were marked by considerable skepticism regarding the need for collegewide standards and practices, some professors maintaining that the conventional criteria of unity, coherence, and point are not always relevant to their disciplines or their pedagogical aims. They would agree that such and such a paper was flawed, even laughably so, and yet still object to the notion that they should design their assignments or grade papers in such a way as to enforce a respect for college writing standards in their students. These questions and demurrers eventually led to the creation of advanced seminars, offered from time to time, in which the forms of discourse are more closely related to various disciplinary aims and practices. (Such seminars are especially important at a time when emphasis is falling more intensely on the resemblances, not the differences, between humanistic and scientific discourse.) Despite failure to arrive at a consensus, the faculty writing seminars have been so popular that today most of the faculty has been accommodated (many professors more than once), and only one seminar each summer is needed to orient new faculty members and first-time tutors to their roles as teachers of writing at Grinnell College.

Writing Lab

In 1972, even before the writing seminars were under way, the college established the Writing Lab in response to the first tutors' request for help with the composition problems of their students. These tutors, many of them nervous and inexperienced in the teaching of composition, referred selected students to the lab for help with grammar and paragraphing. The lab grew quickly, as students came in without referrals and from courses other than the tutorial, for help with papers they were writing. Today the lab has its own centrally located office and a permanent staff comprising three full-time and two part-time instructors holding the rank of lecturer. These instructors, experienced teachers all, were recruited from within the Grinnell community and have either bachelor's or master's degrees, in English, history, education, or art. The lab is open five days a week, from 9 to 4, and serves in a given semester as many as one quarter of the students in residence and several faculty who come in for consultation.

Shortly after its inception, the lab began to offer a one-credit course, graded Pass/Fail, to students who need an individualized program of instruction. (This course can be repeated, for a total of two credits.) Each of these students meets once a week with the same lab instructor, bringing in drafts of work in progress or already graded papers for analysis. Enrollment in this course is generally larger in the fall, as many tutors routinely sign up students who look as though they will need help.

For the past seven years, the lab has offered a four-credit composition course, limited to freshmen and sophomores, which enrolls those who did poorly in the tutorial, as well as a number of other students (many of them foreign) who want the benefits of a highly structured composition course. (The English department offers, once each year, an advanced course in composition. Students who wish to teach English in Iowa secondary schools must either take this course or sign up for a two-hour independent in the Writing Lab where they get experience assisting the director, observing the lab staff at its work, and occasionally taking on a student of their own.)

Currently the lab staff is working to develop uses for the computer in the teaching of composition at Grinnell College. The lab has several VT 100 terminals connected to a mainframe, as well as DEC Rainbows with text-editing capability and attached printers. Lab records are kept on the VT 100s, and the machines are available to the growing number of students who use the computer to compose and edit their papers and prefer conferences at a terminal rather than at the instructor's desk.

Problems

All this activity makes the lab an integral part of campus life, but there are problems involved with its use. The lab defines its responsibility as helping students to improve their skill at stating arguments they have already formulated, which for the most part means instruction in grammar and paragraphing. But it became clear from the start that one cannot teach composition skills by concentrating on only one part of the writing process. Poor writers often need help with substantive matters. They need help getting started or working out the relations among the various ideas that occur to them as they try to respond to an assignment, as well as with grammar and sentence structure. Even the better writers may produce completed drafts that clearly show a misunderstanding of their subject or a mismanagement of their argument, and here too help is needed. Since the lab assigns no papers on its own, the instructor must, in order to teach, make use of those assigned by others, actually laying on hands, helping students to make an outline, tighten a phrase, or sketch in a whole new line of development. Naturally, conflicts arise: on the one hand, the lab instructors, even assuming they have a knowledge of the subject, may be violating the trust of the professor by aiding students in the process of invention; on the other hand, by limiting themselves to advice regarding sentence structure and topic sentences, the instructors may be helping students to achieve mechanical correctness in papers that are unsatisfactory in other respects. Whichever way they go (to state the case in its most extreme terms), the lab instructors place themselves in a false position in relation to the professor, the student, or the instructor's own sense of mission.

To minimize such conflicts, the lab notifies the appropriate professor of a student's first visit and asks for guidance in handling the case. Most of these requests remain unanswered, a sign that the majority of professors at Grinnell are willing, even eager, to have their students accept whatever help the lab can give them. In return, the lab instructors have developed considerable skill, teaching effectively and tactfully enough to justify the professors' trust and the use of their assignments. Only a few students take the one-hour course twice, and most walk-in students learn, in time, to put their ideas together without help. Nevertheless, there still remains an uneasy feeling (as some have expressed it) that the presence of the lab compromises the ideal relation between professor and student, examiner and examinee. This position is not unwarranted, and any college planning a writing lab must be prepared to deal with it.

Other stubborn problems arise in any writing-across-the curriculum program, even when there is no writing lab. Composition is perhaps a more difficult skill to teach than to learn, and professors committed to assuming their share of the collegial burden might wonder whether they are sacrificing their disciplinary aims to the jointly conceived aim of general literacy, in effect making use of the discipline to teach writing, and not the other way around. (This factor makes it difficult sometimes to find Grinnell professors willing to teach designated courses, as they do not get released time for the extra burden.) Even if all professors were enthusiastic, a number of them might still turn out to be poor teachers of composition, no matter how many writing seminars they take or how committed and experienced in other respects they are—an outcome that will not surprise those who have been teaching composition forever and yet know they still have much to learn about it.

Conclusion

At a recent advanced faculty writing seminar, the leader suggested that there might be one way of bringing about good writing without committing the faculty to more involvement in the writing process than it can afford: abolishing the elective system in favor of a structured curriculum that would constitute an implicit acceptance of a developmental model of intellectual growth. Such a system, she suggested, would go some way toward eliminating at least those writing problems that arise from a student's not being ready for a given conceptual task or from not having received the kind of instruction that would bring such readiness about. But the faculty is reluctant to make changes for fear of relinquishing what is most valuable in the present curriculum. At the moment, one of its most valuable features is a writing program that makes writing instruction, at whatever level of need, plentifully available to all students, at a moderate cost to the college and small sacrifice of departmental resources.

Janet Youga
Janice Neuleib
Maurice Scharton

11. Illinois State University Developmental Freshman Program

1. **Department responsible for the writing program: English**

2. **Staffing**

	Regular 101 Fall	Regular 101 Spring	Intensive 101 Fall	Intensive 101 Spring
Part-time faculty members	11%	13%	10%	18%
Graduate students	14%	17%	75%	82%
Full-time instructors	1%	6%	15%	0%
Assistant, associate, or full professors	74%	64%	0%	0%
Members of other departments	0%	0%	0%	0%

3. **Enrollment policy**

	Regular 101 Fall	Regular 101 Spring	Intensive 101 Fall	Intensive 101 Spring
Maximum	23	21	20	20
Minimum	20	20	20	20
Average	22	19	19	17

4. **Program size**

	Regular 101 Fall	Regular 101 Spring	Intensive 101 Fall	Intensive 101 Spring
Number of students enrolled	1,444	1,053	387	189
Number of sections offered	65	53	20	11

Handling freshman composition is one of the most difficult tasks English departments face. In one or two courses, we are expected to meet the needs of almost every student who enters our doors and to make the class flexible enough to accommodate each student's interests and abilities. Perhaps the most challenging part of this task is responding adequately to the needs of high-risk freshmen. These students need special help, and the English department at Illinois State University responded, as most schools did, by offering remedial courses. Although these courses were successful, we still felt some dissatisfaction with the method. Despite our vigorous efforts to create a positive attitude toward the course, students and even some teachers and administrators who should have known better continued to use demeaning labels when referring to the class or its students. Also, the extra semester needed to complete the course put students behind their friends and classmates, thereby eliminating part of their support group that first year and delaying entry into certain courses, majors, and programs.

To help eliminate these problems, we started searching for a way to give the high-risk students the special tutorial instruction they needed without channeling them into a remedial course. We wanted to find a way to combine an introductory writing course with tutorial instruction that was an integral part of that course.

Our solution was the Intensive 101 Program for developmental students. The program has two features that make it both unique and very effective. First, Intensive 101 is a three-credit-hour course that meets five days a week, two days being used for tutorial instruction. Second, each class is taught by one teacher assisted by two undergraduate teaching assistants (UTAs) who handle the extra two days of individualized learning. The teacher meets with the class three days a week (Monday, Wednesday, and Friday) to introduce aims and assignments, discuss rhetorical strategies and writing techniques, and teach skills such as dictionary use, documentation, and summarizing. On the remaining two days, UTAs provide tutorial help for the exercises and assignments and supervise small-group work. Occasionally, UTAs are given a brief lesson to teach, such as résumé format, but their primary duty is to serve as tutors.

It is natural to be skeptical about how much can be accomplished in one semester, even if students meet five days a week. Having switched to this program from one in which students were given the full semester's training before entering 101, we were skeptical ourselves. However, our pre- and post-course tests indicate that intensive students improve at a rate *comparable* to that of our regular 101 students. There is reason to believe, therefore, that we have reduced the high-risk factor associated with this group.

We attribute the program's success to its two unique features, the five-day schedule and the UTAs, but before we could implement these strategies, we needed to decide which students would be placed in the program and which theories of composition would determine the design of the course.

Placement

Our goal in designing a placement test was to determine students' writing abilities, not just their mastery of mechanics or skill in producing "themetalk." The test had to call for a written response to a rhetorical situation and had to be judged on how well the demands of the situation were met. Essay prompts were composed that gave the student a role, an audience, a purpose (expressive, informative, or persuasive), and a scene or context for the communication. The prompts posed questions of personal values in the context of university life and involved deciding which of a pair of responses to a problem was preferable. Three raters trained in holistic grading then evaluated the papers based on the appropriateness of the writer's response to the rhetorical situation. For example, students might be asked to choose between defending a tuition increase or a program in which students perform university service projects to reduce operating costs. As a member of a university committee (role), the student could write an open letter to the committee (scene) trying to persuade (aim) a subgroup within the committee (audience) to support one of the two plans.

Surface errors are not given decisive weight in the evaluation process. The essay evaluation plus the ACT English subscore, which is used to factor students' knowledge of standard written English into the decision, are combined to determine placement. The rhetorical nature of the essay prompt means that students in the intensive program often do not conform to the basic writer paradigm. Intensive students may be proficient at standard English and the five-paragraph theme format but still unable to respond to a rhetorical problem. If they cannot think through a problem and produce discourse that communicates a message to an audience, they are offered the extra help of the Intensive Program.

Theoretical Assumptions

Although we encourage all 101 instructors to use certain teaching strategies, these techniques are absolutely required for our intensive teachers. The course must be process-centered. Students work on one paper for two weeks, being carefully guided through the various stages of the writing process—invention, notes, drafts, conferencing, peer editing, revision, polishing, copyreading, final draft. At first, the teacher intervenes frequently to make sure each step of the process is followed, but as the semester continues, students begin to internalize the process, and teachers interfere less and less in the writer's work. At no time in the semester, though, does the teacher revert to simply collecting finished products; the supervision simply eases up.

Part of this supervision process is conferencing (or "workshopping"), a valuable technique in teaching writing and one that is used for every paper. While students are still working on an early draft, teachers discuss the papers with them to ward off problems and suggest better ways in which to handle the topic. Although this intervention does not guarantee perfect papers, it does mean final drafts are free of basic structural and content problems. It also gives students a chance to find out if they're really communicating what they intended to say, and if not, a chance to alter the way they've expressed their ideas. The process saves teachers an enormous amount of time in at-home grading and correcting and saves students the frustration of feeling they have wasted time and effort and still have not produced what the teacher wants.

However, the role of reader and critic does not belong to the teacher alone. Students need an audience to provide feedback on their ideas and style, and teachers are not always the best audience for every topic. Students learn as much from each other as they do from us about whether something is clear or whether a tone is offensive or whether they are reaching an audience. At least they do after we have taught them to be good peer editors. A technique such as Richard Lanham's Paramedic Method or a peer-editing questionnaire on such items as purpose, audience, voice, detail, organization, and surface errors provides a concrete way for students to help one another improve their papers and clarify the thoughts behind the papers.

Our intensive teachers also know that many of their students have experienced repeated failure in writing classes. These students often have a very low image of themselves as writers and view each paper as yet another opportunity to fail. In this class, therefore, students receive encouragement and positive reinforcement so they will not continue to associate writing with failure and continue to hate it. Since they can only improve their writing through practice, they are encouraged to do this without the threat of being punished for every mistake they make. Students understand that this is not a class where they are expected to know how to write, as they are in their other classes, but where they learn how to write. It is where they gain confidence and not where their history of failure is repeated. This does not mean easy grading. It does mean that students learn to write in a nonthreatening atmosphere, one that is conducive to learning and to developing a positive attitude about writing.

Course Goals and Design

Intensive 101 is designed to develop writers who are (1) skillful and flexible in applying writing skills to problems; (2) able consciously to monitor, analyze, and alter their writing processes; (3) able to edit and evaluate the work of others; and (4) informed concerning the rhetorical tradition and standard written English.

We meet the goal of developing flexibility and skill by encouraging variety in the writing assignments themselves. The course is divided into seven units covering the three primary aims of discourse. Unit 1 focuses on expressive, units 2-4 on informative, and units 5-7 on persuasive discourse. Students must adjust voice, style, and the presentation of material to suit each of the three aims, an activity that demands skill, flexibility, and an awareness of rhetorical strategies. In addition to the papers, students must also keep a journal for summaries and responses to readings, for class notes, and for invention.

To meet the other three goals of the course, we focus on the process of writing. When students must work through notes, heuristics, several drafts, conferencing, and peer editing, they become quite adept at monitoring their own writing. Also, as they practice peer editing themselves, they learn to evaluate the work of others and become skillful at correcting errors in standard written English.

To illustrate how the course works on a daily basis, we have briefly outlined a sample two-week period during which a paper would be produced.

Week 3: Informative Discourse

Day 1: Teacher introduces aim and specific assignment.
Day 2: UTAs introduce invention techniques to help students find topics.
Day 3: Students define their topics.
Day 4: UTAs introduce heuristics to help students generate support or details for their topics.
Day 5: Students write rough drafts.

Week 4

Day 1: Teachers hold conferences with each student while other students revise.
Day 2: Students write second drafts while UTAs are available to answer questions.
Day 3: Students do peer revision of structure, support, voice, etc.
Day 4: Students do peer editing of style.
Day 5: Students proofread final drafts in groups and turn in finished papers.

On days in which the work on the paper does not take up the period or when drafts are done at home, students are assigned readings for discussion from *The Writer's Rhetoric and Handbook* by McMahan and Day or *The Writer's Resource* by Day and McMahan. Students also do several in-class essays to monitor their writing progress when there is no teacher interference.

Turning in the finished paper, then, is only one in a long series of steps students take in the writing process. They see that good writing takes time, thought, effort, feedback, and revision. They are also shown that teachers are interested in every step of the process, from the formulation of an idea to the correction of one last comma, and not just in the final product.

The course is a practical application of the theoretical assumptions behind the program and creates a successful student-oriented, process-centered class. But there is one other important ingredient for success—the UTAs. Without these tutors, the extra help the students need would not be available. The UTAs are the heart of the program.

Undergraduate Teaching Assistants and Training

In selecting UTAs for the intensive program, we look for good writers (not necessarily English majors) and for people who will be sensitive to the needs of struggling freshman writers. To ensure that our UTAs are good writers, we require a B average in all writing courses and across the board. But because sensitivity is also important, we do not always choose the A student over the B. We often find that B students can relate more easily to the writing problems freshmen have because they, too, had to work hard to become good writers.

Teachers in advanced English classes and around campus are asked to watch for students who would make good UTAs and encourage them to apply. In addition to listing GPA and grades in English courses, we ask applicants for a statement about their writing experiences and plans for the future. Two teachers must also write letters of recommendation for the student. Final selection is made by the director of writing and the director of the Writing Center with the approval of the department chair.

Once selected, UTAs must enroll in a 291 course, Undergraduate Teaching Experience, which centers on the work UTAs will do in the intensive classes and in the Writing Center where they also work as tutors. UTAs learn how to provide individualized instruction, diagnosing writing difficulties and finding ways to eliminate these problems. They are also instructed in current writing research so they understand the theoretical framework of the intensive course and in research on individualized learning so they understand the importance of the tutor's role in helping intensive students. Finally, UTAs discuss their responsibilities in the 101 class and are given some instruction in classroom management. UTAs keep a daily journal of their 101 and Writing Center experiences and do a case study of one student's progress during the semester.

In the intensive classroom each teacher is assigned two UTAs to handle the Tuesday-Thursday classes. The teacher retains primary responsibility for the course, but the three act as a team for the benefit of the students. UTAs support and reinforce what teachers say and are available in class or in the Writing Center for individual help.

We have found that there are many benefits to this system of instruction. Students are the first to benefit because they have two additional experienced writers to answer their questions and help solve their problems. Students receive more time, more individual attention, more tutoring, and more experienced reader responses. Since UTAs also work in the Writing Center, they are available for additional help if their students need it, thus reducing the problem of a lab tutor's trying to interpret what the 101 teacher wants.

Intensive teachers also benefit from UTA assistance. Instructors can concentrate on teaching important rhetorical strategies and writing techniques, knowing the UTA will reinforce each lesson in addition to handling minor problems teachers often have no time for.

The Intensive Program also provides great teaching experience for the UTAs themselves. They have the opportunity to learn about the profession in a situation less threatening than student teaching. Since UTAs work in pairs, they never have to face the class alone and always have the teacher within easy reach if they need help. The tutorial situation helps ease them into the classroom but still puts them in a situation where they are providing real, concrete help to students who most need it. Feeling a sense of accomplishment is something UTAs often speak about.

Finally, we feel that using UTAs is good for the teaching profession. Our program gives UTAs the opportunity to experience the nonmonetary rewards of the profession, to have that sense of accomplishment. Watching a good teacher at work and actually handling a class also alleviates much of the fear many UTAs have about teaching. The positive attitude and confidence they gain can turn good UTAs into good colleagues.

The benefits to students, teachers, UTAs, and the profession make this part of the program well worth the effort and the cost. UTA services are relatively inexpensive but can still strain department budgets. We are fortunate to have a college that supports writing at all levels and across all disciplines and therefore provided an extra $20,000 for UTA salaries.

Program Uniformity

Splitting the 101 program into regular and intensive sections caused some initial concern. As anyone who has taught developmental students knows, losing perspective on grading standards for these students is easy, especially if theirs are the only papers being read that semester. To ensure uniformity among all 101 teachers (regular, intensive, and UTAs), the department developed grading standards that clearly explain the meaning of each grade and began to hold grading sessions several times a semester for all 101 instructors.

The grading standards seem self-explanatory, but we find that not all teachers interpret them exactly the same way. So, periodically during the semester, we assemble to compare our interpretations and try to unify our standards. Before a grading session, three student papers are distributed to all 101 teachers and UTAs who then grade them. Both intensive and regular 101 papers are used but are not identified as such. At the session, the tallied results are discussed and teachers are invited to explain their evaluations. Through the discussion, the group tries to come to some consensus about the grade each paper should receive. It does not always work. We find that emotional topics, such as abortion, can produce A through F responses. However, the group session forces teachers to confront their own topic biases by keeping the discussion focused solely on the grading standards. "I disagree with the student's stand on this issue" is not accepted as valid criticism of the student's writing. The sessions also force teachers to focus on the importance of creating effective assignments since disagreements often tend to be centered on the assignment rather than the paper.

Looking Ahead

We are very pleased with the success of the program and have found its basic structure so sound that we can focus our attention on minor revisions rather than on a new draft. Improvements we hope to make may serve as cautions for any department trying to implement such a system.

The theoretical assumptions and course design of the program are crucial to its success. Teachers who are selected to work in the program must subscribe to its philosophy and agree to follow its syllabus. This limits the freedom of each teacher to a certain extent, but since modern research and our own testing support the value of these methods, we feel justified in making the demands.

Our grading sessions also taught us an unexpected lesson about teacher selection. We were worried about our UTAs losing perspective on standards because of their inexperience. However, because of the training they had received in the 291 course, the UTAs' grades were more consistent within their group and more closely connected to the grading standards than were those of either the intensive or the regular 101 teachers. We have, therefore, concluded that it would be better for the program if most of the teachers were graduate students being trained in our writing program. They would be studying the theory and pedagogical techniques of the intensive program in their courses and still be under some supervision themselves as the UTAs are now.

UTAs are a great help to teachers, but they also are an added responsibility. Teachers must be willing to meet their UTAs before the class begins and regularly thereafter. They must make UTAs aware of lesson plans well in advance so the assistants know what is expected of them and how they fit into the overall design of the course. Teachers must also make it clear to students that all three of their instructors are responsible for the course and the grading. The three must appear as a cohesive group, and while not usurping the authority of the teacher, UTAs must also have some authority that students recognize. For example, teachers might be responsible for grading major assignments while UTAs handle journals. Also, attendance and participation should be required all five days. Students must never feel that only one teacher's evaluation counts.

UTAs must also be selected carefully and must understand their duties and responsibilities. Though they are full-time students feeling the usual pressure that a full course load brings, they must understand that they are responsible for two class periods a week and must come prepared to handle them. They must also understand that they are the heart of the program and that we depend on them for its success.

Finally, both teachers and UTAs must be compatible coworkers who are willing to put forth the effort necessary to make the program work. Teachers must take the time to discover and make use of the talents and strengths of their UTAs, and UTAs, for their part, must listen to and learn from the supervising teacher. The three must function as a team and operate for the common good of their students. Ultimately, our goal must not be to provide assistance for our teachers or experience for our UTAs but to provide the best possible writing class for our students.

Allison Wilson

12. Jackson State University
Composition and Literature Sequence

1. Department responsible for the writing program: English

2. Staffing (varies; figures below are for 1983–84 only)

Number of freshman composition courses taught by part-time faculty members	0
Number taught by graduate students	0
Number taught by full-time instructors	4
Number taught by an assistant professor	1
Number taught by a full-time member of a department other than English	1

3. Enrollment policy (for 1983–84 only)

Maximum enrollment	32
Minimum enrollment	14
Average enrollment	30

4. Program size

Number of students enrolled in the freshman composition program

fall 1983	112
spring 1984	74

Number of sections of freshman composition offered

fall 1983	4
spring 1984	3

Jackson State University's department of English offers three two-semester sequences of freshman courses, two of which—Composition and Literature (104-105) and Composition and Literature for Honors Students (111x-112x)—are intended primarily to improve the written language performance of beginning college students. Composition and Literature for Language Arts Majors and Minors (111-112), of which I was appointed coordinator in 1980, is intended not only to serve this general purpose but also to provide instruction in the kind of critical analysis that is the staple of upper-level courses in English, foreign languages, speech, drama, and mass communications. The original course materials consisted only of Harry Shaw's *A Complete Course in Freshman English*, which was used in 111; X. J. Kennedy's *Literature: An Introduction to Fiction, Poetry, and Drama*, which was used in 112;

and any books individual instructors chose to include. Exposure to these materials was considered sufficient preparation for all future communicative tasks.

It recently became necessary, however, for those juniors entering teacher education programs in Mississippi's state-supported institutions to present satisfactory scores on the College Outcome Measures Project (COMP), a measure that requires students to respond in a variety of formats to a variety of media. For Jackson State's predominantly black student body—many of whom come from neighborhoods where black dialect is spoken and from public school systems that are overcrowded, understaffed, and underfunded—this test has presented difficulty, primarily because students have had little opportunity to develop proficiency in oral or written standard English. Unfortunately, the adverse conditions prevailing in many public schools also exist to some extent in Jackson State's English department: there is no official policy concerning maximum enrollment per class; many instructors teach five courses per semester; and the department is often unable to provide materials.

Program Assumptions

I therefore found it necessary during the summer of 1983 to restructure English 111-112 not only to provide sufficient opportunity to develop varied communication skills but to maintain original, pre-COMP goals as well. I hoped also to compensate for large student load and class size by including small-group and one-to-one activities and to offset the shortage of materials both by selecting textbooks that supplied a wide variety of information and by using those audiovisuals already available in the library's media center. The program was, furthermore, designed with the following assumptions in mind:

1. *Exposure to a variety of ideas presented from a variety of viewpoints seems more likely to encourage divergent thinking than does total immersion in the kinds of egocentric, almost therapeutic reminiscences and reflections advocated by those who naively equate creativity with spontaneity.* This is not to say, however, that personal experiences, evaluations, and interpretations are of no importance in the freshman classroom or that the social, cultural, political, and economic concerns of isolated factions should be devalued or dismissed. It is, on the contrary, this very understanding of larger contexts and broader perspectives that often leads to the objective examination of previously unquestioned beliefs and therefore to the formulation of novel approaches to familiar issues.

2. *Exposure to a variety of thematically organized media seems more likely to promote genuine involvement, and thus effective communication, than does total dependence on the printed page.* The enhancement of reading skills should probably take precedence over other forms of literacy, primarily because the ability to read critically is both of immediate use in classroom and testing situations and of long-range benefit in many professions to which college graduates aspire. Both in and out of the educational setting, however, one must often process information acquired through media other than those emphasized in the traditional freshman English classroom. To introduce these nontraditional materials in any but an integrated, thematic arrangement, furthermore, seems unwise, in that a medium-by-medium organization cannot but add impetus to

the common notion that ideas presented in one form are more or less valid, more or less useful, or, above all, more or less subject to scrutiny than are those presented through some other medium.

3. *Writing assignments that are argumentative or persuasive and that contain a research component seem more likely to develop critical abilities than do assignments that elicit unexamined, unqualified, and unsupported descriptive, narrative, and expository writing.* To classify assignments on the basis of the traditional modes, or any modes for that matter, can, in fact, create a distorted view of written texts that can actually block original thought. Such a stance can easily lead to the conclusion that each type of writing exists exclusively in a pure and inviolate state—that description and narration (being personal and impressionistic) and exposition (being "factual") are exempt from clear, logical presentation and, far worse, that argumentation or persuasion precludes the creative use of description, narration, and exposition. Thus, while spontaneous emotive or regurgitative writing may serve as a valuable prewriting activity by suggesting areas and avenues of exploration, major writing assignments for college-level courses—if these courses are intended for any purpose other than the invocation and articulation of what is already known—must encourage assimilation of and response to diverse ideas and perspectives.

4. *Writing assignments that grow naturally from a series of diverse prewriting and revision activities seem more likely to result in effective and purposeful communication than will those that have no clear connection to preliminary contemplation and reader response.* Freedom from the autocratic teacher-student dichotomy, as reflected in the traditional lecture-and-evaluation format, is therefore essential both to the development of content and to the discovery of form.

5. *Traditional oral and written exercises, quizzes, and examinations seem more likely to influence final written products favorably if timed and selected with the relevant student population in mind.* Under no circumstances, however, should the mastery of materials designed to improve or evaluate isolated grammatical, mechanical, reasoning, or test-taking skills be permitted to take precedence over, or serve as a prerequisite to, the examination, generation, and written articulation of ideas. For even standard English proficiency is of little use in the absence of a message to be communicated.

6. *Instructors who are free to formulate and sequence activities and assignments in response to student ability and interest are more likely themselves to become involved in the communication process and therefore to provide positive role models than are those forced to adhere to a rigid schedule and inflexible list of common materials.* It is important, however, that instructors, whether experienced or inexperienced, be familiar with and in favor of program goals as specified and that they be aware of available instructional aids.

Problems and Strengths

Weaknesses in the present structure of Composition and Literature for Language Arts Majors and Minors are, for the most part, practical. Few available classrooms, for instance, are ideal for the kinds of group and one-to-one encounters that help develop a concept of audience and create an atmosphere conducive to objective criticism. Thus, valuable instructional time is often abbreviated by the need to arrange and rearrange desks, an inconvenience that increases as class enrollment increases. What is worse, burgeoning enthusiasm is sometimes checked by the need to avoid disturbing other students and classes.

The problem of staffing and faculty orientation is, however, far more critical, in that the list of 111-112 instructors, which varies from semester to semester and which may or may not include the coordinator, is sometimes amended even after classes have begun. Faculty members have little opportunity to build on the experience of previous semesters or to develop a genuine interest in the program and its goals. Some instructors, in fact, have little opportunity even to become familiar with these goals before they must begin selecting materials and sequencing activities, a dilemma that could have an indirect negative effect on students. Inconsistencies in the distribution of overall student load and in the scheduling of courses has a more direct negative effect, in that some students, because of sheer numbers, are provided less opportunity for individual attention and many, because second-semester 112 courses are not always offered at the same hours or taught by the same instructors as first-semester 111 courses, do not have the option to continue their studies with an instructor who is aware of their talents and shortcomings.

But such mundane matters, though worthy of attention, are far outweighed by the strengths of English 111-112, which are reflected primarily in the often profound change in student attitude both toward written communication and toward the thoughtful consideration of ideas that often must precede effective written communication. Students no longer see reading activities, for instance, as one-dimensional dead-end searches for minor details to be underlined and memorized, nor do they any longer see other forms of media as mere fillers for slow days. Rather, they are far more inclined to approach various ideas, regardless of origin, not as "right" or "wrong" answers to hypothetical questions but as useful material that itself raises real issues to which there are, like as not, no all-purpose responses at all—an attitude change that is also reflected in students' own writing processes and products. And although this change by no means produces instant texts of professional quality, it does cause a gradual but definite disappearance of the kind of trite, timid, academic formula writing characteristic of student writers who work in a vacuum and who, therefore, can conceive of no audience other than the single-minded, tradition-bound teacher stereotype. Most students also experience a gradual and sometimes hard-won shift in their attitudes toward error, as they begin to understand not only that surface correctness, particularly standard English correctness, does not compensate for shallow exploration, inappropriate support, and chaotic presentation but also that concentration on written standard English morphemes and syntactic units is often counterproductive or even debilitating during the early stages of a writing assignment. Furthermore, these various attitudinal changes usually give students an increased confidence in their ability to generate and effectively to present written material, a confidence without which little purposeful communication can take place.

Appendix

Program Description

Composition and Literature for Language Arts Majors and Minors (English 111-112) is designed to improve the reading, writing, speaking, and test-taking skills of freshman English, foreign language, speech, drama, and mass communications majors and minors. English 111-112 replaces Composition and Literature (English 104-105), the regular freshman sequence. Objectives, textbooks, and supplementary reading materials for English 111 are listed below.

Program Design (111)
Objectives

1. Students will read/view essays, short stories, poems, photographs, films, and videotapes. Specifically, students will
   a. differentiate shades of meaning;
   b. distinguish between literal and symbolic meaning;
   c. recognize purpose, main idea, supporting detail, causal relationship, and sequence of events;
   d. distinguish fact from opinion, implication, assumption, and inference;
   e. distinguish between information and misinformation, relevance and irrelevance, logic and illogic, completeness and incompleteness;
   f. recognize implications for new approaches or solutions to real-life issues;
   g. relate written ideas to ideas presented through other media;
   h. relate ideas presented through various media to personal, cultural, and societal values.

2. Students will prepare argumentative or persuasive essays. Specifically, students will
   a. use conventional grammatical forms, punctuation marks, spellings, and citations;
   b. use a variety of sentence and paragraph patterns;
   c. describe, and comment on, real-life situations, making value judgments where appropriate;
   d. summarize and react critically to ideas presented through various media;
   e. use imagination, experience, controlled observation, statements from authorities, and statistical data to generate sufficient supporting details;
   f. identify legitimate grounds for argument;
   g. reason inductively and deductively while avoiding common logical fallacies;
   h. relate assumptions and conclusions to supporting details;
   i. test conclusions where applicable.

3. Students will participate in large-group, small-group, and one-to-one discussions and, where applicable, present essays orally. Specifically, students will
   a. use conventional grammatical forms and pronunciations;
   b. speak clearly and audibly while using appropriate stresses, pauses, and gestures;
   c. use vocabulary, syntax, details, and examples appropriate to audience, occasion, and purpose;

d. recognize logical fallacies and irrelevant information;
   e. lead, as well as participate in, discussions;
   f. ask as well as answer questions.

4. Students will respond appropriately in testing situations. Specifically, students will
   a. follow written and/or spoken directions;
   b. use question sheets, answer sheets, and writing materials similar to those used in standardized testing;
   c. complete tests and examinations within the time allotted.

Textbooks

Vincent Barry, *Good Reason for Writing*
Glenn Leggett, C. David Mead, and William Charrat, *Prentice-Hall Handbook for Writers*
Marcia Stubbs and Sylvan Barnet, eds., *The Little, Brown Reader*

Supplementary Reading Materials

Novels, biographies, and similar materials selected by the individual instructor on the basis of student interest and capability.

Margot Soven

13. La Salle University Freshman Composition Program

1. Department responsible for the writing program: English and Communication Arts

2. **Staffing**

Percentage of freshman composition courses taught by part-time faculty members	8%
Percentage taught by graduate students	0%
Percentage taught by full-time instructors	0%
Percentage taught by assistant, associate, and full professors	92%
Percentage taught by full-time members of departments other than English	0%

3. **Enrollment policy**

Maximum enrollment	22
Minimum enrollment	11
Average enrollment	21

4. **Program size**

   Number of students enrolled in the freshman composition program
fall 1983	478
spring 1984	234

   Number of sections of freshman composition offered
fall 1983	21
spring 1984	11

At present, students at La Salle University are required to take only one writing course. The chair of the English department appoints the staff for the course, and a Writing Program Committee is responsible for evaluating it, suggesting changes, and conducting faculty development related to teaching the course. As part of a universitywide curriculum change, the existing course has recently been modified, and a new course for underprepared students will be added to the program.

History

The required freshman composition course has evolved over the last four years. In 1980, the English department, dissatisfied with the freshman composition course, initiated a study of its curriculum to address the following problems: many students disliked the course, instructors complained it was difficult to teach, and many instructors thought that it wasn't effective. After fairly extensive review, using faculty surveys as well as recent theory on teaching composition, the department developed new guidelines for the course. Prior to this review, the course had been traditional: structured on the traditional rhetorical "modes," it included at least eight papers as well as a research paper. The teacher questionnaire revealed that instructors were frustrated trying to fit everything in and that they were not emphasizing the writing process. The new guidelines attempted to deal with both problems. Teachers were urged to abandon the research paper, to reduce the number of required papers to six, and to teach prewriting, drafting, and revising strategies. It was also suggested that they experiment with alternatives to the modes for structuring assignments and try out new instructional formats such as in-class conferencing and peer review.

The objectives for the course remained pretty much the same. We continued to emphasize generic writing skills related to the personal expository or argumentative essay. The revised guidelines, however, now included the following statements: "Attention should be focused on the *act of writing itself* as well as on the finished product. Students should improve in their ability to use prewriting, drafting and revising strategies."

The department strongly believed, and still does, that instructors should have the freedom to design a course that capitalizes on their strengths and experience and meets the needs of their individual classes. Therefore, adoption of a single text was not advised. The department recommended several process-oriented texts and urged instructors to choose the one most compatible with their own teaching style.

Administrative changes included the appointment of the present Writing Program Committee, which examines and recommends new textbooks, evaluates the writing program, and periodically conducts faculty workshops. Previously these activities had been conducted informally and sporadically.

In a sense the 1981 course change was a child of its time. Research on the composing process and on its obvious implications for pedagogy attracted our attention and led us to hope that the modifications in our program would both lead to better writing in the course and teach strategies for composing that students could transfer to writing tasks encountered in their other courses. We hoped that both students and teachers alike would find the course more purposeful and would therefore be more pleased with it.

Students and teachers have indicated in various surveys that the new course is more successful than the old. However, like its ancestor, the new course is undergoing revision in response to new developments in writing pedagogy and to the persistent feeling (which seems to reach a climax just about every three years) that we could teach writing more effectively than we are now.

The English department has been strongly influenced by writing-across-the-curriculum theory, with its dual emphasis on writing as a mode of learning and on the importance of familiarizing students with the genres of writing common to different disciplines. During the last three years we have conducted a successful writing-across-the-curriculum project at La Salle. One result of the project is that both teachers of composition and teachers of other subjects have begun to question the relevance of a freshman composition course that focuses exclusively on the personal essay and uses the traditional modes for structuring assignments. We are listening more attentively to students who say that they do not see the connection between our freshman writing course and the writing they are assigned in other courses.

To strengthen that connection, we have had to reconsider the kinds of papers we assign and reexamine our present use of readings in the composition class. Instead of using readings as stimuli for ideas to be used in a personal essay, we see the need to emphasize the use of readings as sources of information. Accordingly, we plan to provide explicit instruction in extracting information from a text for the purpose of writing about it. In the same vein, we plan to reintroduce the formal research paper into the freshman course.

During the past three years we have become more concerned about our weakest writers. Many on the faculty believe that a single required course, even when augmented by individual tutoring in our writing center, does not provide sufficient instruction for these students. The latest revision of our writing program, described below, addresses this problem as well.

The New Program

The new composition program tries to address these concerns. It includes: (1) a requirement of two composition courses for the weakest writers; (2) an emphasis on the kinds of writing tasks and genres that will be required of students in their other courses; (3) assignments that use writing to help students learn to write about written materials; (4) an introduction to library sources and basic research techniques; and (5) continued emphasis on the writing process and on basic rhetorical skills.

The existing course has been renamed College Writing II. We have added a new course, College Writing I, which our weakest students must take. To develop these two courses we drew on three texts: *Writing in the Arts and Sciences* (Maimon et al.), *Writing and Reading across the Curriculum* (Behrens and Rosen), and *The Informed Writer* (Bazerman). Maimon's text is useful for its descriptions of discipline-specific assignments, such as the report. Behrens's text provides readings from different disciplines for students to write about. Teachers may also choose one of the similar readers on the market such as *Readings in the Arts and Sciences* (Maimon et al.) and *Fields of Writing* (Comley et al.). Bazerman's text, *The Informed Writer*, which considers the writing course as a vehicle for introducing students to the "informed conversation" of their disciplines, provides a theoretical rationale and a method for teaching students how to write about written materials.

We have found the Bazerman text useful in Writing and Reading across the Curriculum II because it has helped us shape writing assignments that closely resemble the writing tasks given in content courses that require students to write about written materials. By focusing on the development of informed ideas based on information gathered from reading, this text provides a new, radically different persona for the composition course.

Teaching composing skills is no longer limited to teaching students how to make meaning from personal reflection. Bazerman says,

> If as teachers of writing we want to prepare our students to enter into the written interchanges of their chosen discipline and the various discussion of personal and public interest we must cultivate various techniques of absorbing, reformulating, commenting, and using reading. ("A Relationship" 658)

He reminds us that traditionally these skills were subsumed in the research paper assignments but were not given "careful explicit attention." Composition instructors limited instruction to information gathering and to the process of relating new comments to previously written materials but rarely dealt with the *extraction* of information from the materials. To help students understand not only the claims of a text but the purpose and audience for which it was written, Bazerman recommends paraphrase, summary, and analysis of the purpose and technique of documents. He points out that "particular writing assignments can help students become more perceptive readers and can help break down the tendency toward vague inarticulateness resulting from purely private reading" ("A Relationship" 658).

The assignments are followed by exercises in annotation and informal response, which let students explore their own assumptions about texts. Students learn to use writing as a mode of learning as well as of communication. They move on to writing reviews in which they evaluate a text in relation to its intended purpose, observable reality, and other texts. And finally, Bazerman advocates offering students the opportunity to define issues and develop informed views on original theses, a task that involves the integration of all former modes of responding to texts.

In addition to writing four short papers based on assignments in the Bazerman text and exercises in summary and paraphrase, students write an essay about fiction, a report based on primary observation, and a research project that includes writing a proposal and an annotated bibliography. Rhetorical skills are taught within this context as they apply to the given document. For example, when students write the research paper, they are provided with examples of several ways of writing the introduction; when they write the critique, methods of conclusion are discussed. Sentence structure and grammatical conventions are taken up as needed. The traditional modes are introduced as methods of organizing and developing ideas.

Our new course, College Writing I, includes specific instruction in basic rhetorical skills, on the assumption that students who take this course need additional work in writing sentences, paragraphs, and the basic structure of the essay. However, students in the course will also begin to work on paraphrase, summary, and library skills. Approximately twenty-five percent of our freshmen will be required to take both composition courses. For placement we will use a formula based on SAT and TSWE scores and grade-point averages.

Problems Related to Implementing the New Program

We foresee two possible problems in implementing the new program. First, some instructors may be reluctant to make the change to the new course structure and curriculum. Those who feel most strongly that all of our students need instruction in basic rhetorical skills will have the most difficulty adopting the new program. Second, the new course may begin to suffer from overload. Some instructors may attempt to teach the generic writing skills of the old curriculum as well as the skills incorporated in the new curriculum.

We will try to help our faculty by offering workshops on the rationale for the course, at which materials developed by the three instructors who have piloted the course will be distributed. We intend to evaluate the new program informally on an ongoing basis and perhaps formally at the end of three years. At this point we are sure it will be an improvement on our current program. However, if past experience is a guide, it will take only two to three years for problems and difficulties to emerge. Faculty members will once again remark on how difficult it is to teach writing, at which time....

Mary Fuller
Donald A. Daiker

14. Miami University Freshman Composition Program

1. **Department responsible for the writing program:** English

2. **Staffing**

Percentage of freshman composition courses taught by part-time faculty members	10%
Percentage taught by graduate students	32%
Percentage taught by full-time instructors	6%
Percentage taught by assistant, associate, and full professors	52%
Percentage taught by full-time members of departments other than English	0%

3. **Enrollment policy**

Maximum enrollment	28
Minimum enrollment	NA
Average enrollment	26

4. **Program size**

   Number of students enrolled in the freshman composition program
fall 1983	2956
spring 1984	2816

   Number of sections of freshman composition offered
fall 1983	115
spring 1984	112

A Basis in Research

Miami University's freshman composition program, which consists of a semester course in composition (English 111) and a semester course in composition and literature (English 112), is based on the results of experimental research conducted at the university.

Sentence combining became an important component of English 111 following an experimental study funded by the Exxon Education Foundation. The study showed that college freshmen trained for a semester in sentence-combining techniques wrote essays that experienced college composition teachers judged superior to essays written by conventionally trained college freshmen.

The curriculum for English 112, Composition and Literature, has also been established through experimental research. With support from the National Endowment for the Humanities, we designed and tested a course in which reading and writing assignments were carefully balanced and in which equal time was allotted to the interpretation of literature and the discussion of student writing. When this course was favorably evaluated both by its instructors and by consultant Donald J. Gray of Indiana University, the principle of integrated instruction in composition and literature became central to the curriculum for English 112.

Current topics for research at Miami University include protocol analysis, the team grading of writing, the "epistemic" approach to the teaching of composition, and writing across the curriculum. It seems likely, therefore, that experimental research will continue to influence the university's freshman composition program in important ways.

The First-Semester Course

Serving approximately 3,200 freshmen each year, the freshman composition sequence comprises the only required courses for all students entering Miami University. Students scoring a 27 verbal and 28 composite on their ACT (or 600 verbal and 600 quantitative on their SAT) may enroll for English 115, the honors writing class. Most freshmen, however, enter English 111, a course focusing on the students' writing and on the composing process.

Although any experienced faculty member or graduate teaching assistant may design and teach an independent syllabus, most instructors in the department teach the standard process-oriented syllabus, which places students' writing at the center of the curriculum. No rhetoric or handbook is required. In fact, the students' writing—paragraphs, prewriting assignments, sentence-combining exercises, preliminary drafts, and formal papers—serves as the major text of the sixteen-week course. Students complete a writing assignment for each class meeting and, once in class, continue writing or share their writing in large or small group discussions.

The syllabus roughly follows a two-week, six-class cycle. On the first day of a unit, the teacher assigns a paper, spending the day with freewriting and prewriting activities to help students discover subject matter, explore their ideas, and—in some cases—actually begin to draft papers. To the second and fifth class meetings students bring sentence-combining exercises that they have completed in their notebooks. At the third and sixth meetings students participate in workshops, sharing excerpts or full rough drafts of their formal paper assignments. At the fourth the teacher spends the full hour returning and discussing the graded papers from the previous unit. Finally, at the seventh class meeting, teachers collect final papers and begin the cycle anew.

The workshops help strengthen the focus on student writing and the composing process. We want students to learn that writing is a way to discover the content and shape of their written work and to challenge and test their ideas. When they draft and share their writing in the workshops, they learn that composing is a recursive process involving thinking, planning, writing, and rewriting. While the specific workshops focus on various elements of writing—on learning and applying revision strategies, on developing and shaping ideas, on finding authentic voice—each workshop reinforces the students' control over their own words.

Sentence Combining

A unique and powerful feature of our standard syllabus involves sentence-combining exercises, due the second and fifth meetings within each unit. Before class, students complete a basic sentence or full discourse exercise from *The Writer's Options*, a sentence-combining textbook by Donald A. Daiker, Andrew Kerek, and Max Morenberg. The text resulted from the original Exxon-funded experiment at Miami. Through their work in *Options*, students learn basic constructions like participles, absolutes, appositives; practice using subordination and coordination; and complete whole-discourse exercises in selecting pertinent and vivid details, organizing ideas, developing a central idea, and creating appropriate voice and tone. Students bring their work to class in notebooks, but usually discussion and class activities focus on samples that selected students write on the blackboard or reproduce with the use of ditto masters. Another favorite activity among the students is to work in groups on individual exercises and share them with the class on overhead transparencies.

On the fourth day, students receive their graded essays from previous units. They spend most of the hour discussing samples of outstanding papers from the graded set, which the teacher normally reproduces and distributes to the class. If teachers choose, they devote part of the class time to teaching specific elements of writing. Some may focus on developing and maintaining coherence, others on matters of usage, others on eliminating wordiness. Whatever the focus, though, all questions and issues emerge from the students' writing itself.

Teacher Training

Freshman composition is taught by approximately sixty full-time and forty part-time instructors. All new graduate assistants are required to attend a three-week sprint course, The Theory and Practice of Teaching Composition, which meets daily during the three weeks directly preceding the fall semester. The course, which carries four hours of credit and provides $300 stipends to offset living expenses, trains the apprentice teachers in cognitive psychology and language development, in relations between reading and writing, in the composing process, in evaluation research, and in practical classroom pedagogy, such as establishing and running workshops and responding to student writing. At the end, the graduate assistants are better prepared either to teach the standard syllabus or to create an independent syllabus that places the students' writing and composing processes squarely at the heart of the course.

The Second-Semester Course

For well over twenty years the second semester of Miami University's freshman composition sequence—English 112, Composition and Literature—

had been a course in which instruction in literature overwhelmed instruction in writing. Even the standard syllabus for the course reflected this imbalance: for every writing assignment, there were at least five reading assignments; for every class period set aside for discussing and evaluating student writing, there were at least five periods given over to interpreting literature. And although experienced instructors traditionally had been free to replace the standard syllabus with one of their own, they invariably changed only titles—a different short story here, a new poem there—and not the structure of the course or the relation between literature and composition. Indeed, the dominance of literature became so pronounced that the director of freshman English asked in a departmental memorandum, "Does the emphasis on literature in the course actually impede the teaching of writing?"

In response to this problem, three faculty members—aided by a grant from the National Endowment for the Humanities—designed a course that carefully integrates the teaching of composition with the teaching of literature. The syllabus for that NEH course has now become the standard syllabus for English 112. Its central principle is that reading and writing reinforce and sustain each other.

The new standard syllabus balances literature assignments with composition assignments and discussion of literary works with discussion of student writing. Thus every two-week unit consists of three reading assignments balanced by three writing assignments and of three classes focused on the interpretation of literature balanced by three classes focused on student writing. To achieve this integration, the new syllabus includes fewer literary works than in the past. Last semester, for example, the only assigned works of literature were four short stories (by Steinbeck, Glaspell, Fitzgerald, and Cheever), a single novel (a choice of *The Sun Also Rises* or *The Great Gatsby*), and a group of poems by one writer (a choice of Emily Dickinson or Adrienne Rich). But the integrated syllabus does more than simply reduce reading and increase writing. It complements the seven formal papers with a wide range of shorter writing activities.

The shorter writing assignments, all directly relevant to the assigned literature, include prewriting activities like nonstop writing, looping, listing, and brainstorming, which help students in the discovery process. Perhaps even more important are three kinds of paragraph assignments. The explanatory paragraph asks students to recognize, select, and organize evidence in support of a generalization implicit in the literary work. These assignments provide practice in familiar strategies for paragraph development, especially illustration, comparison and contrast, and cause and effect. The argument paragraph asks students to examine the text in ways that lead to or reveal an interpretation against one of equal or nearly equal validity. To do this, students must learn to recognize and anticipate objections to their argument—a valuable exercise in improving both their persuasive writing and their literary understanding. A third kind of paragraph assignment asks students to show how their personal response to a particular character or event affects their perception and evaluation of a work.

Additional writing practice is provided by sentence-combining exercises that vary in both length and function. The sentence-level exercise helps students learn to control useful constructions like appositives and participles, absolutes and noun clauses, as well as to practice relevant tasks like documenting their sources of information and working quotations from the text into their own sentences. The paragraph-level combining exercise is designed to help students understand and use important critical terms like *irony, symbol, setting, point of view, rhythm,* and *metaphor*. Another type of whole-discourse exercise asks students to select from a group of sentences only those most relevant to their purpose and then to organize them into an effective whole. Still other exercises provide a decombined version of a passage from a story or novel and ask the students to combine the sentence elements and then compare their recombined version with the original. This kind of exercise not only gives them a more intimate sense of the author's style but demonstrates how changes in word order and grammatical form can sometimes change or modify meaning.

The full-draft workshops, prewriting activities, paragraph assignments, and sentence-combining exercises provide a learn-as-you-write introduction to literary method and practice. More importantly, they provide the foundation for full-length compositions and thus encourage students to view writing as a coherent sequence of tasks. When Donald J. Gray evaluated the integrated course for the National Endowment for the Humanities, he found it "markedly successful both in improving students' writing and in increasing students' literary understanding."

Conclusion

Enthusiasm and professional excitement—though intangible qualities—are key elements of our freshman writing program. Our students benefit, we believe, because the atmosphere at Miami is conducive to composition research and pedagogy. All members of our English department faculty teach writing, and all are invited to attend monthly seminars on composition. A number of us consider rhetoric and composition our major professional commitment. We pursue scholarship in writing theory and pedagogy, participate regularly in professional meetings, and collaborate frequently on composition-related research. The department now offers an MA, MAT, and PhD with concentration in composition and rhetoric. Miami University is the home of the Ohio Writing Project, the first site of the Bay Area–National Writing Project in Ohio. The Miami University Center for the Study of Writing, whose members come from mass communication, systems analysis, math, and teacher education as well as from English, meets regularly to hear reports on its members' current research projects, to review papers and grant proposals, and to discuss issues related to teaching composition. Over the last few years, our department has hosted two international conferences on sentence combining—featuring such speakers as Peter Elbow, Joseph Williams, Donald Murray, William Strong, and James Kinneavy—and it has sponsored visits from Donald Graves, Toby Fulwiler, James Moffett, Linda Flower, E. D. Hirsch, and others. It is not surprising, then, that our freshman writing program reflects our active research interests and our school's support of those interests. At Miami we are excited about teaching composition, and that excitement ensures that we will continue to scrutinize and evaluate our freshman composition program.

Diana L. George

15. Michigan Technological University Freshman English Program

1. **Department responsible for the writing program: Humanities**

2. **Staffing**

Percentage of freshman composition courses taught by part-time faculty members	55%
Percentage taught by graduate students	1%
Percentage taught by full-time instructors	0%
Percentage taught by assistant, associate, and full professors	44%
Percentage taught by full-time members of departments other than English	0%

3. **Enrollment policy**

Maximum enrollment	28
Minimum enrollment	10
Average enrollment	23

4. **Program size**

    Number of students enrolled in the freshman composition program
fall 1983	1341
spring 1984	1097

    Number of sections of freshman composition offered
fall 1983	57
spring 1984	48

Program Description

Michigan Technological University's freshman English program is intimately tied to its writing-across-the-curriculum program in both theory and practice. The work of scholars such as James Britton, James Moffett, and Janet Emig informs the thinking of the Tech faculty members in their writing courses. The faculty is heavily process-oriented, as is evident in the way the courses are taught.

Faculty members are encouraged to use frequent informal and ungraded writing-related exercises in class, such as student-journal assignments; small-group meetings to share journal entries, generate topics, or critique drafts; freewrites to start or end class; brainstorming sessions to generate assignments; and other such techniques to encourage a good deal of writing and talking about that writing.

Even though guidelines outline the basic program in freshman English, the department neither provides nor encourages a common syllabus. MTU composition faculty members are active scholars and researchers in the field, and thus the program offers a strong variety of approaches to composition teaching.

Some instructors, for example, have combined their interests in composition research with their knowledge of theories of reading and interpretation. The result has been a cluster of courses based on reader-response theory, taught by four faculty members. Other faculty members, strongly influenced by the work of Donald Murray, Ken Bruffee, and others, have turned their classrooms into workshops and emphasize the teaching of revision and peer response in their approaches.

Because this is such a varied and active faculty, the department does not assign one set of texts for the three-course sequence. The only text required throughout the sequence is a handbook. Currently, the department is using the *Harbrace Handbook*.

The freshman English requirement is nine hours of humanities coursework, normally taken in the freshman year. The three-course sequence (101-102-103) is divided into segments designed for specific writing tasks and levels of difficulty.

Writing across the Curriculum

Because the Department of Humanities believes strongly in the writing-across-the-curriculum concept, that program has been a mainstay of writing instruction at MTU. Besides the basic nine-hour freshman English sequence, students are exposed to writing instruction throughout their tenure at the university.

To achieve that end, writing-across-the-curriculum workshops introduce the basic concept—that writing is a mode of learning—to faculty members in other disciplines. These workshops emphasize the role of writing in developing critical thinking and language skills, and those who attend the workshops are encouraged to use writing in classes throughout the curriculum at MTU. The kind of writing most encouraged is exploratory and ungraded, the kind of writing James Britton calls writing that is "close to the self." This writing allows students to make knowledge their own, to struggle with questions, and to depend constantly on written language as a means of knowing.

The writing-across-the-curriculum program is, then, an integral part of the department's writing program. Through it, students continue writing instruction beyond the conclusion of their freshman year. They also continue to learn how writing can be used throughout their lives as a learning tool.

One practical result of the writing-across-the-curriculum approach has been the collaboration of humanities faculty members with those in other disciplines. Humanities instructors have, for example, worked with biologists and mathematicians to help design writing components for these classes.

The Freshman Sequence

HU 101

This course, like most introductory composition courses, focuses primarily on writing that is close to freshman students' experiences. Instructors often teach personal narratives and descriptions, but the course is not limited by a rhetorical format. It is, however, a course that focuses on the personal. Instructors generally make heavy use of student journals and group reading and critiquing sessions.

Since MTU runs on a ten-week-quarter system, no more than three major papers are generally assigned in any of the three courses. All these papers, however, move through draft stages with the guidance of group critiques and the instructor's written and oral feedback.

HU 102

The second course in the freshman English sequence generally focuses on a more difficult kind of writing and thinking. Students should be exposed to some kind of research-writing task. That research need not take the form of the traditional research paper as it has generally been taught in English departments, but it should expose students to writing that is "outside the self," writing that may be difficult at first to process. To that end, students are generally introduced to library work, to hunting for topics and essays within the constraints of the library, and to deriving information from the material they find.

Though assignments in this second course tend to be more formal and more difficult, faculty members still rely on those techniques used in 101. That is, students are generally encouraged to keep a journal, to share their work with their peers, to meet frequently with their instructor, and to understand their own composing and revising process.

HU 103

This third course is often seen as a combination of writing course and introduction to humanities. In this quarter, students generally read literary texts or work with music, art, popular culture, or philosophy. The aim is to encourage personal and critical responses to the humanities.

Reading and writing assignments vary with the instructor, but the aim in every section is to expand our students' abilities in reading and critical thinking and to give them a brief introduction to possibilities in humanistic studies.

Advanced Placement

No student at Michigan Technological University is exempt from the nine-hour freshman English requirement, but the humanities department offers an advanced placement program for those students who have scored 26 or higher on the verbal section of the ACT or 600 or higher on the SAT. These students are assigned to an honors section of HU 101 (HU 101H). Students achieving a grade of B or better in HU 101H will be allowed to replace HU 102 and HU 103 with six hours of upper-division humanities courses (excluding performance courses).

Since the humanities department is the center of writing-across-the-curriculum activities on this campus, the academic courses it offers in all disciplines of the humanities are writing-intensive courses. That is, faculty members in English, philosophy, art, foreign languages, music, film, and theater are encouraged to use the same techniques for teaching their discipline as composition instructors use to teach theirs. Journals, peer critiques, frequent rewrites, and other techniques are used in these courses as well, since the faculty firmly believes that writing is not merely a skill but a way of knowing, a way of learning.

Honors students may opt to finish their freshman English requirement by taking two of these courses.

Teacher Training

The freshman English faculty engages in a series of seminars designed to share recent research in the field and to explore areas of needed research. Both part-time and full-time staff members attend these seminars.

The Writing Center

In addition to classroom instruction, the Department of Humanities, through the writing center, provides tutorial assistance for students who need or want it. The writing center uses students' work as the basis of instruction and relies very little on self-paced work of any sort.

Tutors in the writing center are professionals rather than peer tutors. They work with students in one-on-one conference situations throughout the term. Although drop-in hours are available, most student hours are scheduled so that a student will sign up for a tutor and work with that tutor throughout the term.

In addition to conferencing, tutors run short courses in grammar and spelling and a special course in vocabulary for biology students.

The focus of the writing center is not remediation. Most of the work done in the center strengthens skills in critical thinking, development, and organization.

Conclusion

The Department of Humanities' writing program at Michigan Technological University is characterized by the strong integration of current composition theory into all levels of writing instruction. The writing center, the writing-across-the-curriculum workshops, and the basic freshman English program all work together to create a coherent program through all levels of university teaching.

16. New York University Expository Writing Program

1. Department responsible for the writing program: English

2. Staffing

Percentage of freshman composition courses taught by part-time faculty members	0%
Percentage taught by graduate students	97%
Percentage taught by full-time instructors	0%
Percentage taught by assistant, associate, and full professors	3%
Percentage taught by full-time members of departments other than English (½ of the above 3%)	50%

3. Enrollment policy

Maximum enrollment	15
Minimum enrollment	12
Average enrollment	15

4. Program size

Number of students enrolled in the freshman composition program

fall 1983	2,300
spring 1984	2,100

Number of sections of freshman composition offered

fall 1983	160
spring 1984	145

Administrative Background

The Expository Writing Program of New York University, an interschool program serving the university's four undergraduate colleges, was established in 1978 to offer preparation in writing for all New York University students. As the largest private university in the country, New York University attracts a diverse range of students. The average verbal SAT score of entering freshmen is 550. All students are required to take two semesters of expository writing (Writing Workshops I and II) and to pass a proficiency exam before graduation. There are no exemptions. Students who believe they are excellent writers (who are recommended by an instructor or who score over 650 on the verbal portion of the SAT) may take one of the honors sections. International students or students for whom English is their second language may take a series of equivalent courses if they so choose or if their proficiency in English warrants such a program. (The English as a Second Language sequence comes after the basic language courses offered by the American Language Institute and is a 1½-year requirement rather than a one-year course of study.) The Expository Writing Program also houses the Writing Center, a free tutorial service in writing for the entire university. The Writing Center is staffed by twelve graduate students, each of whom also teaches one section of the writing workshop courses. In the spring semester fifteen undergraduates serve as peer tutors, as part of the requirement for an honors section of Writing Workshop II (Peer Tutoring).

The Expository Writing Program is housed within the English department of the College of Arts and Science. The director and one of the assistant directors are faculty members of this department. The director is a tenured associate professor; the assistant director, a tenured associate professor. The other assistant director, who is also the director of the Writing Center, holds a joint appointment in the English department and in the Program in English Education. She, too, is a tenured associate professor. Faculty members from both the Department of English and the Program in English Education serve as faculty mentors to the program and regularly teach a section of Writing Workshop I or II.

Course Description

Writing Workshops I and II are designed as a year-long course of study, although the students are in different sections with different instructors each term. The classes are limited to fifteen students and meet an hour and fifteen minutes twice a week. There are a few night classes, which meet for two and one-half hours once a week. Writing Workshop I focuses on the development of critical reading and writing abilities. Students are asked to engage in sequences of writing assignments in which they are invited to experiment with point of view, with voice, and with various modes of inquiry. The course progresses from writing about the self, to writing about the world, to writing about texts. Early in the semester, students are given a diagnostic exam, a writing task similar to the proficiency exam administered at the completion of Writing Workshop II. Teachers go over the results of the diagnostic exam so that students can prepare for the proficiency exam and other writing tasks under testing conditions. In order to develop our students' analytical and interpretive abilities, we have them engage also in a series of critical reading activities, which provide stimulus for most of the students' writing assignments. Students are encouraged through reading logs to keep track of their personal transactions with a work—to raise questions, to make connections, to explore other possibilities, to offer conflicting perceptions. At times, students may read and respond to one another's writing, raising similar questions that suggest revision. Teachers' commentary on writing comes on early drafts, where students can use the questions and judgments of an experienced reader to stimulate further revision of their work. By the end of the term, students have written at least six completed papers, through several revisions, of three to five pages. Many have also kept journals and have written abstracts, summaries, a résumé, a letter of application, and short exploratory pieces.

Writing Workshop II focuses on the writing demands of the various disciplines and on processes of inquiry and research. Students apply their critical reading abilities to texts of major thinkers in various disciplines and discover the kinds of questions and concerns that shape differing fields of study. They also write in response to questions they pose within the framework of scientific and humanistic inquiry. The course requires no less than five essays of five to ten pages in multiple drafts; one essay must include library research and documentation. Students also learn how to write under exam conditions. Many students keep learning journals during the semester, recording informal responses to ideas raised in class and through discussions of papers. As in the previous semester, teachers' response to students' work comes on early drafts and is designed to stimulate revision.

The textbooks for both writing workshop courses have changed many times since the start of the program. Books have been chosen primarily for the kinds of readings or information available rather than for the teaching apparatus implied by each. Most recently we have used *The Norton Reader* (ed. Eastman et al.) for the first semester and added a writing-across-the-curriculum reader the second semester. We also have students purchase a handbook. We have experimented with rhetoric textbooks but have not found one suitable to our needs. We find that the students' own writing should be the focus of instruction.

Staff and Training

The Expository Writing Program is staffed principally by graduate teaching assistants (usually around eighty a semester) selected on a competitive basis from applicants from any graduate program in the university. Although approximately one-half of the teaching assistants (preceptors) come from the Department of English or the Program in English Education, others come from history, American civilization, performance studies, media ecology, and Near Eastern Studies, to name a few. All new preceptors must attend a two-day orientation to the program and must take for credit a graduate course in the teaching of writing during their first term teaching in the Expository Writing Program. The course, taught by a faculty member in English education, focuses on the most current theory and methodology. During past semesters our preceptors have read works by Ken Macrorie, William Coles, Peter Elbow, Nancy Sommers, Sondra Perl, James Britton, and Nancy Martin, among others; they work through a series of assignments, including a case study of themselves as writers and a tape recording, transcription, and analysis of ten minutes of themselves teaching writing. Beyond the practicum, the directors of the Expository Writing Program offer workshops during the semester on such topics as responding to student writing, evaluating writing, and working with ESL students. The preceptors are also invited to attend a faculty colloquium on writing, which has brought to New York University Ann Berthoff, Elaine Maimon, Ann Raimes, Stanley Fish, Louise Rosenblatt, J. Hillis Miller, Robert Weiss, and others.

Conclusion

The Expository Writing Program continues to develop every year, adjusting to the best theory of composing and the teaching of writing available to us.

We have begun to research the use of word processing in the teaching of writing and have just completed a year-long investigation of teacher-student writing conferences within the program. Each year we have several dissertations, supervised by the faculty in English education, on various aspects of the program: the composing process of ESL students, a description of peer-group talk about writing, methods of teacher response to student writing, and a description of how teachers read students' texts. In all of our efforts we attempt to meet the needs of our students, and while doing so, we hope we can also address the needs of our professional community as well.

John A. Perron, CSC

17. St. Edward's University Freshman Studies Program

1. Department responsible for the writing program: Universitywide

2. Staffing

Percentage of freshman composition courses taught by part-time faculty members	47%
Percentage taught by graduate students	0%
Percentage taught by full-time instructors	0%
Percentage taught by assistant, associate, and full professors	53%
Percentage taught by full-time members of departments other than English	0%

3. Enrollment policy

	Freshman Studies	English 13
Maximum enrollment	35	25
Minimum enrollment	30	10
Average enrollment	33	23

4. Program size

Number of students enrolled in the freshman composition program
- fall 1983   456
- spring 1984   420

Number of sections of freshman composition offered
- fall 1983   17
- spring 1983   17

Course Descriptions

St. Edward's University requires two semesters of freshman composition. The ordinary sequence for most freshmen is Freshman Studies and English 13. On the basis of testing conducted during orientation, about seventy percent of entering freshmen bypass developmental writing and enroll in the six-semester-hour interdisciplinary course called Freshman Studies. This one-semester program, offered only in fall semesters, integrates two three-hour courses: Humanities 10 (Introduction to Humanities) and English 10 (Rhetoric and Composition I). The second-semester composition course is English 13 (Analysis and Composition II). These two courses will be described below.

Freshman Studies

From its inauguration in 1975, Freshman Studies has had the following objectives: to provide freshmen with a common educational experience, to assist them in making the transition from high school to college, and to introduce them to the curricular goals of St. Edward's University. To achieve the third objective, Freshman Studies fosters exploration in a variety of subject areas; illustrates the relations between academic disciplines; encourages integration of conceptual learning with lived experience; and assists students to reason critically, communicate effectively, and examine the values they live by. Since 1975 the course has assumed several different formats as its planners have attempted to achieve these objectives. Nevertheless, Freshman Studies has always tried to integrate an introduction to the humanities and sciences with instruction and practice in composition. Faculty collaboration in course planning has been a hallmark of the program, and faculty members from a variety of academic disciplines continue to teach the course.

So that students in the course will perceive Freshman Studies as a shared educational experience, the course is designed to ensure that the students encounter the same subject matter, receive comparable instruction and practice in rhetoric and composition, and engage in similar learning activities. To make the connections between topics clear, the major theme of the course is "The Human Person and the Liberal Arts and Sciences," and all course work is related to this theme. To achieve cohesion between presentation of subject matter and practice in composition, we have adopted a paradigm of the process of inquiry (see Young, Becker, and Pike) as the underlying principle of unification for the course. Presenters of subject matter show how the process of inquiry applies to their topic, and students use this process of inquiry to generate ideas and content for their compositions.

The Humanities 10 portion of Freshman Studies is a lecture course divided into four three-week modules on the self, the family, the body politic, and the environment or the future. Four lecturers from such departments as theology, philosophy, political science, and biological sciences design and present these units. The lecturers are responsible for sequencing lecture content, selecting appropriate readings, formulating discussion questions pertaining to both lectures and readings, devising value-analysis exercises, and providing the knowledge students require to complete their writing assignments. Lecturers are also responsible for pointing out connections between their units and the course theme, the process of inquiry, and the other units of study.

Currently module 1 draws on the disciplines of psychology and theology. Its theme is "The Experience of Becoming a Person." Lectures present a Jungian approach to this subject, and readings include Robert Johnson's *He* and Madonna Kolbenschlag's *Kiss Sleeping Beauty Good-bye.*

Module 2 draws on sociology and literature. Its theme is "The Human Person in the Family." Lectures explicate Erik Erikson's stages of psychosocial development and apply these to the novel students read for this unit, Rudolfo Anaya's *Bless Me, Ultima.*

Module 3 employs political science. Its theme is "The Human Person as Decision Maker in the Body Politic." Lectures cover a variety of related topics: political insiders and outsiders, classical liberalism and conservatism, the issue of who rules in America, the problem of how to verify the effectiveness of public policymaking. Students read *The Autobiography of Malcolm X*, and the lecturer contrasts Malcolm's response with the approach taken by Martin Luther King. Students discuss articles on who rules America and on influential Texans, and they study the consequences of Brown v. the Board of Education of Topeka, Kansas, via the CBS documentary report *Blacks in America: "With All Deliberate Speed"*?

Module 4 draws on the natural sciences. Its theme is "The Human Person as Discoverer." Lectures and readings explain the scientific method, expose the pseudo-conflicts between humanities and science, and take up the issue of genetic engineering. In preceding years, the topic has been "The Human Person and the Environment" and "The Human Person and the Future."

In the English 10 portion of Freshman Studies, students employ the lecture materials as the basis of discussions, value analysis, and written assignments. Instructors are usually from the English department and are assisted by an intern of junior or senior class standing. In addition to following up the lecture portion of Freshman Studies, these instructors are responsible for explaining and implementing the rhetoric and composition program the faculty has adopted. The basic text is our own *Freshman Studies Handbook*, which explains the rationale and objectives of the course, shows how the process of inquiry may be applied during the writing process, provides a syllabus for the course, and includes space for note-taking during each lecture. This text is supplemented by Janice M. Lauer et al., *The Four Worlds of Writing*.

As explained and illustrated in these texts, student writing arises from the stages of the inquiry process. That is, students articulate cognitive or felt dissonance, systematically explore their questions or subjects using a modified version of tagmemic heuristics, explain their insights, and test alternative hypotheses. They record this writing on specially designed worksheets, on which space is available also for their analyses of occasion, audience, aim, and methods of essay development. Peer evaluation of essay drafts aids revision. In addition to discussion of humanities content, it is by means of student practice with the inquiry process, the tagmemic heuristics, and the aims and modes of discourse (from James L. Kinneavy) that we try to develop powers of reasoning and imagination.

For modules 1 and 2 students write papers with expressive aim. Chapters 1 and 2 of *The Four Worlds* are easily adapted to the content of these modules. For modules 3 and 4 students write papers with persuasive aims, using chapters 3 and 4 of *The Four Worlds*. Over the course of the semester, students also write three in-class essays on assigned topics. Individual instructors evaluate their students' out-of-class essays, using scoring sheets adopted from Texas A&M University, but they do not evaluate their own students' in-class essays. Other instructors score these holistically in group-scoring sessions. These writing assignments and several value-analysis exercises provide students with occasions to relate course content to their own experience.

A student's final grade in Humanities 10 is the average of the student's grades on four module exams, quizzes on reading assignments, class participation, and a library project. For their library projects, students draw names of persons connected with some public issue related to one of the four modules. Students present the results of their library search on specially designed answer sheets, in a one-page essay, and in an oral report to their class.

To pass English 10 a student must write at a defined minimal level of competence on a holistically scored final essay. If a student writes an acceptable essay (students with a course average of C or higher are eligible to write a second time if they fail the first), then the student's final grade in English 10 is the average of the student's grades on the four module essays, the invention and revision work on these essays, the three in-class essays, class participation and quizzes, and the end-of-course essay. If a student fails to write an acceptable essay at the end of the semester, then a student may receive a grade of F or No Pass, depending on the student's average for completed course work. To progress to English 13, students enrolled in English 10 must achieve a C or higher, as well as write an acceptable postcourse essay.

Freshman Studies meets from 9 to 11 a.m. on Mondays, Wednesdays, and Fridays. Humanities 10 lectures are given on Mondays and Wednesdays to one-half of the freshmen at a time. English 10 is divided into six or seven sections of thirty to thirty-five students each; half of these sections convene before their humanities lectures and half following the lectures. On Fridays, English 10 sections meet from 9 to 11 for concentrated instruction and practice in composition, called Writing Workshop. Faculty and interns meet weekly to discuss course content, assignments, and classroom activities.

Student evaluations of Freshman Studies have been highly favorable since 1979. Between seventy and ninety percent of participants say the program is cohesive, fosters exploration, clarifies their values, and improves their writing, reasoning, listening, and note-taking skills. Since 1980, after a developmental English sequence for deficiently prepared students was implemented, ninety to one hundred percent of the freshmen have successfully completed both portions of the course.

English 13

English 13 is the required second-semester composition course. Instructors from the English faculty are responsible for ten sections of this three-hour course, limited to twenty-five students and offered at various times on Monday-Wednesday-Friday and Tuesday-Thursday sequences. Although course format and scheduling appear traditional, the rhetorical approach taken in English 13 is, according to Clinton S. Bùrhans's categories, "contemporary" rather than "traditional." Course objectives are to provide students with continued instruction and practice in the process of composing introduced in English 10 and to introduce them to various kinds of referential writing.

Students continue to apply the inquiry process to writing; use a modified version of tagmemic heuristics during exploration; analyze the occasion, audience, and purpose of writing; and engage in peer evaluation at various times in the writing process to assist invention or revision. They record invention work, essay planning, and peer evaluation on specially designed worksheets. Work with Kinneavy's four modes continues, but students concentrate on writing that aims to be informative or to prove a thesis. Reading student and professional compositions provides occasions for discourse analysis.

English 13 requires three in-class essays on assigned topics; four out-of-class essays, one of which is a controlled research paper; and an acceptable postcourse essay. Procedures for grading these compositions and computing the final course grade are the same as those of English 10.

Texts for this course are Janice M. Lauer et al., *The Four Worlds of Writing*; Boyd Litzinger, ed., *The Heath Reader*; and Gibaldi and Achtert, *MLA Handbook*. John M. Wasson's *Subject and Structure: An Anthology for Writers* has also been used.

Unit 1 of English 13 is on education. Selections from the reader are assigned, as well as chapter 6 of *The Four Worlds*. Students compare viewpoints from the readings and define *education*. In the major paper for this unit, students evaluate some viewpoint on education.

Unit 2 results in a critical paper on a literary work. Students use chapter 7 in *The Four Worlds*, with instructors providing a supplementary exploratory guide for short stories. Students read and discuss fiction and poetry assigned from the reader.

Unit 3 is the controlled research paper. Students employ chapter 5 in *The Four Worlds* and the *MLA Handbook*. The faculty selects a topic for this unit project, for example, "The American Dream," "The Future," "The Impact of Humans on the Environment." Students must work only with the sources provided by the reader or by handouts. Our purpose for such control is two-fold: to teach students how to utilize references for supporting their own insights and how to avoid plagiarism. Despite the control, students have produced essays of definition, causal analysis, comparison and contrast, chronological shifts in meaning, proof of thesis.

Unit 4 is the feasibility report, treated in chapter 8 of *The Four Worlds*. Selecting some campus problem to solve, students address the person who can implement the solution. During this unit, students also receive instruction in oral reports and deliver their reports to their class.

To satisfy the university's freshman-level writing proficiency requirement, students must receive a grade of C or better in English 10 and in English 13 and write an acceptable end-of-the-year essay at the conclusion of English 13.

In January, the English 13 faculty plans the course. During the semester faculty members meet weekly to determine unit assignments, classroom activities, in-class essay topics, and so on.

Student evaluations of English 13 are generally positive. As a rule faculty members who have been at St. Edward's University for several semesters are highly rated. The course is judged valuable and the instruction superior.

Strengths

1. Made possible through Title III funding, collaboration with such nationally prominent academicians as Charles Muscatine, James Kinneavy, Richard Young, Janice Lauer, Frank J. D'Angelo, and Wallace Lambert has facilitated faculty and program development.
2. The composition faculty has formulated a coherent rhetorical framework for a sequential, cumulative, and comprehensive writing program. By the end of the freshman year students have been introduced to Kinneavy's four modes and three aims of discourse (literary aim is reserved for elective courses), prepared for writing in other courses, acquainted with the process of inquiry, and thus prepared for the problem-solving approach taken in the required upper-division writing course, Research and Critical Missions.

3. Freshman courses emphasize writing as a mode of learning and as a cross-disciplinary activity.
4. The establishment of universitywide writing competence examinations, the holistic scoring of these essays according to the procedures developed by Educational Testing Service, and the defined levels of performance required to pass each writing class have improved the quality of student writing, in the judgment of both faculty and students.
5. The diversity of the writing sequence (labs and developmental, freshman-level, senior-level, and elective courses), with provisions for foreign as well as native students, allows students with varying levels of writing proficiency to enter the university and to progress successfully to the level of proficiency expected of a college graduate.
6. Faculty development and adoption of departmental syllabi and grading practices have achieved coherence and consistency across composition sections.

Problems

1. Financial constraints have forced too great a reliance on part-time instructors.
2. Current faculty workload inhibits a systematic preparation of the student interns assisting instructors of freshman composition.
3. Instruction and practice in alternative invention strategies are currently limited to elective composition courses.
4. Despite our efforts, a significant number of foreign students experience difficulty meeting university writing requirements at the upper level, particularly the junior-level competence exam.

Peter Elbow
Pat Belanoff

18. State University of New York, Stony Brook Portfolio-Based Evaluation Program

1. Department responsible for the writing program: English

2. Staffing

Percentage of freshman composition courses taught by part-time faculty members	16%
Percentage taught by graduate students	82%
Percentage taught by full-time instructors	0%
Percentage taught by assistant, associate, and full professors	2%
Percentage taught by full-time members of departments other than English	0%

3. Enrollment policy

Maximum enrollment	25	
Minimum enrollment	15	
Average enrollment	22	(25 in English 101, 15 in English 100)

4. Program size

Number of students enrolled in the freshman composition program
  fall 1983   1,000
  spring 1984 1,000

Number of sections of freshman composition offered
  fall 1983   50 in English 101, 4 in English 100
  spring 1984 Same

We seek here to give an accurate and practical description of a portfolio-based evaluation system we have just instituted. But we can be more accurate and practical if we avoid giving a static picture and instead suggest the inevitable historical flux: the experiments that preceded this system and the inevitable opportunities for modification in the future.

An Instructive History of Writing Evaluation

In the early years of the university (less than thirty years ago) the writing requirement at Stony Brook was a two-semester freshman course taught almost entirely by faculty members in the English department. Then, in the late 1960s, the requirement was reduced to a one-semester course. With the rapid expansion of the university, and one thing and another, that course began to be taught largely by graduate students. Before long, the limit of twenty students per section in writing courses was raised to twenty-five. All the while, writing skills of entering freshmen were probably declining.

Throughout this period, the crucial evaluative decision about proficiency in writing was in the hands of individual teachers—first faculty members, then TAs. It was assumed that teachers would not pass students who were not proficient—who could not write well enough for college or well enough for other university writing assignments.

In the mid-70s faculty members from around the university began to complain that students came to them who had passed the required writing course but who nevertheless were unable to write acceptably. In response to this problem a proficiency exam was put in place in 1977. Passing the course no longer satisfied the writing requirement; the requirement was to pass the exam. With this change, the crucial decision about proficiency in writing was taken out of the hands of the individual teacher and given to examiners who did not know the student.

The goal of the proficiency exam was not just to reduce inconsistency in grading but in particular to keep up standards—or even push them up. Proficiency exams are inevitably attempts at quality control aimed not just at students but also at teachers. The Stony Brook exam, still a requirement for juniors and seniors who entered the university under that legislation, gives students two hours to write a persuasive or argumentative exam from a choice of three questions.

Though the exam was instituted as a move toward increased rigor, the legislation allowed students who passed it on entrance (it was given as a placement instrument) to be exempted from taking a writing course. Thus ironically, over the years (because of various factors, some of them economic), the exam ended up serving to exempt more and more students from any instruction at all in writing.

Standing back and looking at this story, we are struck with the idea that perhaps there would never have been a need for this added procedure for evaluating writing (a procedure in addition to individual teachers giving grades) if the university had still provided two semesters of instruction—particularly if they were taught by faculty members. Might this be true generally? That we get more evaluation of writing as we get less instruction?

Problems with Proficiency Exams

As so many schools are discovering, proficiency exams have problems. First of all, there is serious doubt as to whether they do the very thing they are supposed to do, that is, accurately measure proficiency in writing. The research movement that gives high marks to holistic scoring for validity (but see Charmey) also shows that no matter how accurately we may evaluate any sample of a student's writing, we lose all that accuracy if we go on to infer the student's actual proficiency in writing from just that single sample. We cannot get a trustworthy picture of a student's writing proficiency unless we look at several samples produced on several days in several modes or genres. That is, not only may students not perform up to capacity on any one occasion, there is no one generic thing we can call "writing" (see Cooper). Besides, faculty members continue to complain about the lack of skill in students who pass the exam.

And even if proficiency exams gave a perfectly accurate measure of writing proficiency, they seriously undermine, by their nature, our teaching of writing and send a damaging message about the writing process. A proficiency test tells students that they can do their best writing (demonstrate their proficiency) with fifteen minutes of thought on some issue just sprung on them, followed by writing, followed (sometimes) by some cosmetic revising and copyediting. No drafts, no discussion of the issue with others, no trying out drafts on readers, no getting responses. Surely few of us ever write anything that matters to us in this fashion. But students who pass are encouraged to believe that they can write anything this way, and students who fail are encouraged to believe this is the process they need to learn.

In addition, when a proficiency exam embodies a university requirement, the whole university can be seen as saying to students, "Here's a serious matter (single-parent families, care of the elderly, the relation of books in the real world). Tell us what you think about it in approximately five hundred words; we know you can give it the attention it deserves; and then you can go home." The writing is unconnected to the study of any material and cut off from connection with any ongoing conversation. Is that how we want students to approach serious intellectual issues?

In short, our experience as teachers and our knowledge of recent research in the field made us uncomfortable with the proficiency exam we found in place here. We also began to notice at conferences that others, too, often introduced accounts of their proficiency exams with a disclaimer and some slight gesture of embarrassment.

Thus we began to experiment with portfolios to evaluate writing—portfolios prepared in a writing class but read by outside readers. We were looking for a kind of quality control—not only to avoid inconsistency but to hold up standards (for we do not disagree with this goal behind proficiency exams)—yet also for a way to avoid the problems of proficiency exams. For four semesters we experimented with a relatively small number of sections. In the fall of 1984, along with a new university writing requirement we'd been working for, we made portfolios an official procedure in all sections of EGC 101. The new requirement says that every student must get a C or higher in 101 or else take it again. The portfolio system says that no students can get a C unless their portfolios have been judged worth a C not only by their teacher but also by at least one other teacher who does not know them.

Brief Overview of the Portfolio System

Our handout for all students in 101 is useful here for an overview:

> The portfolio system gives you a chance to satisfy the University writing requirement on the basis of your best writing, writing you have had a chance to think about and revise, and it helps us increase consistency in grading.

At the end of the semester you will submit a portfolio of writing from the course: three revised pieces and one in-class piece. These will be judged by examiners who don't know you: 101 teachers other than your own. In order to get a C or higher in the course, your portfolio must pass. You must repeat the course if you do not get a C or higher. (Note that you are not *guaranteed* a C if your portfolio passes; your grade may be pulled down by other factors such as missing classes, or missing deadlines, or consistently unsatisfactory work on assignments.)

At mid-semester you get a chance for a trial dry run on one paper. If it passes, that counts: include it in your final portfolio as it stands (though you may revise if you wish). If it fails, you can revise it and resubmit it in the final portfolio.

Each paper must have an informal but typed introductory cover sheet that explains what you were trying to accomplish and describes some of your writing process, e.g., what feedback you got and what changes you made in revising.

Portfolios will fail if they contain more than a very few mistakes in grammar, punctuation, spelling, or typing. You will also fail if you have more than a few sentences that are so tangled that the meaning is unclear to a general reader on first reading. This level of correctness and clarity may be harder for some of you to achieve than for others—especially those of you who come to English as a second language. But we insist on it because you all *can* achieve it: you all have a chance for feedback and careful revising.

The examiners must be confident that the work you submit is really yours. This is why we ask for an in-class piece of writing on which you've had no help. Instructors will not forward portfolios to the examiners unless they are confident it is *your* work—and thus will insist on seeing lots of your in-class writing and also insist on seeing the successive drafts of all your writing. They won't accept new pieces on new topics at the last moment that you haven't worked on earlier as part of the course.

The Three Revised Pieces

(1) A narrative, descriptive, expressive piece, or an informal essay. The emphasis is on writing from your own experience. (Fiction is fine, not poetry.)

(2) An academic essay of *any* sort—except for one restriction: the essay must be organized around a main point, not just organized as a narrative or description or a rendering of experience. Thus, for piece #1, you could write an informal essay that just tells a story with a "moral" added at the end—or just describes a scene with a brief conclusion at the end. Such essays can be excellent writing, but for category #2 we are insisting on a different kind of essay—one that most university professors require when they assign writing in a subject matter course: an essay organized in terms of an idea (such as a claim you are arguing for) or an intellectual task (such as comparing, contrasting, defining, or analyzing).

(3) An academic essay which analyzes another essay: that tells *what it is saying* and *how it functions* or *how effectively it says it*. You might analyze a newspaper editorial, a published essay, an essay written by someone in your small group, or you might even analyze one of your own essays. This is practice in close reading and in being able to explain how prose works on readers.

Modes of Writing

We've continually adjusted and tinkered with the kinds of writing we ask for, trying to embody the commitments we stand for as a program, yet trying not to hem in teachers too much.

Modes 2 and 3 above obviously represent our commitment to academic discourse, to the kinds of writing that other faculty members will assign. Indeed we suggest that teachers might want a paper that students could use in another course for mode 2.

Mode 1 represents our strong commitment to imaginative or expressive writing—writing that tries to render or communicate one's own experience rather than explain or analyze it. We feel this mode of writing is currently under attack as inappropriate at the university level. But as Britton shows, expressive writing is the matrix from which skill in other modes derives; English departments are committed to the *study* of imaginative writing as perhaps the best expression of the human spirit; and personal or creative writing is the only mode through which most students can become sufficiently excited with writing to keep it up when not obliged to write—which is the only way they'll ever become genuinely skilled. If we don't give students practice in this kind of writing, no one else in the university will.

We've had some misunderstandings about the distinction between the kind of informal essay acceptable for mode 1 and the more formal one required for modes 2 and 3: teachers occasionally tell students that an essay fits the latter categories when readers feel it does not. We've been reluctant to emphasize words like *formal* and *academic* because of what they often do to student prose. Probably we should talk more about audience and the discourse of various communities.

Some teachers like to use category 1 for the mid-semester dry run: they want to start with what is easier and more fun and build up to what is harder. Other teachers use category 2 or 3 for the dry run in order to get an early start on what usually needs more work and to prevent overconfidence about mid-semester results. Out of this dilemma rise some current experiments in using more than one dry run piece.

We decided not to evaluate the cover sheets: they must be there but students are not penalized if they are done poorly. We made this decision because we are committed to the usefulness of the process writing or "metawriting" called for by cover sheets, yet we don't want to emphasize it too much for students or teachers who hate it. Also we want to reduce as much as possible what readers have to evaluate. Cover sheets are more for students and teachers than for outside readers—though when the writing is borderline it can help the reader to look at them. And readers are invited to allow them to count favorably in borderline cases.

Similarly, poor in-class writing does not count against a student (though we don't much talk about that to students). It represents a symbolic guard against plagiarism. Our main guard is that the individual teachers should not forward writing they are not confident of. Again we let it count favorably in borderline cases. This decision represents our desire not to penalize students for writing they've not had a chance to revise (though some would say that our view does not pay enough heed to "exam writing" as an important mode that students need practice in).

The Evaluation Process

At mid-semester teachers meet to discuss sample papers and agree on some verdicts—a "calibration" session. Then teachers distribute their students' actual mid-semester dry run papers to each other for a reading. The judgment is a simple binary Yes or No, Pass or Fail, worth a C or not. No comments or marks are made on the papers (except to circle unambiguous mistakes in mechanics—especially if a paper fails for that reason). A brief comment is paperclipped to failing papers—usually only a few sentences. (It is not the job of readers to diagnose or teach—only to judge. It is the teacher's job to interpret these comments to the student when necessary.)

If the teacher agrees with the verdict, the process is finished—and this is the case with most papers. But a teacher who disagrees can ask for a second reading from another reader. If that second reading is the same, the teacher can either go along with the two readers or else seek a third reading to validate his or her perception. However, the stakes are not high at mid-semester. A failure doesn't count against anyone, as this is a time for teachers and students to get used to the process; in fact, teachers tend to prefer stern verdicts at mid-semester to make sure students are not lulled into false security.

At the end of the semester the evaluation process is repeated but with full portfolios: the calibration meeting with sample portfolios; first, second, and occasionally third readings; comments only on failed portfolios. Again judgments are binary, and we treat portfolios more or less as a whole instead of making separate verdicts on each paper. (We say that a portfolio shouldn't pass if one paper is definitively weak even if the others are very strong, but we purposely leave this matter somewhat inexplicit, believing that there needs to be room for judgment here.) But this time the gun is loaded: a student whose portfolio fails must repeat the course. Nevertheless, if the two concurring readers agree that the failure is due to one paper, the student may revise that paper and resubmit the portfolio. We treat the inevitable appeals to our office from students the way we treat appeals about grades. That is, we consent to hear stories or read papers when it seems important, for we feel we must be as loyal to students as to teachers. On those occasions when we see something genuinely out of line (rather than just a reasonable verdict that we might have called differently), we go back to the teacher or reader or group and ask them to look again—perhaps saying nothing more, perhaps telling our sense of the difficulty.

Note that though there is a lot of machinery, we try hard to keep it as quick and simple as possible. Because judgments are only Yes or No (instead of 1 through 4 or 6 as with most holistic scoring), because we read portfolios as a whole giving only one verdict, and because there are no comments except brief ones on failing portfolios, readings are surprisingly fast. Many strong portfolios can be read very quickly—some of the papers even skimmed.

An Emphasis on Small Collaborative Groups of Teachers

Small groups of teachers are presently the main vehicle for the functioning of the portfolio system. We invite teachers to form into their own groups of four or five according to friendship or interest (and we group those who prefer random groupings). These groups meet to read papers from each others' classes at mid-semester and portfolios at the end of the semester. They decide on their own specific deadlines and on which of the three kinds of paper should come in at mid-semester (or decide to disagree—allowing a mixed bag of genres). Some groups decide to require a second dry run paper three-quarters through the semester—or to ask for two papers at a slightly late mid-semester date (in an effort to give students more sense of how they are doing).

A few teachers have complained that we give too much autonomy to the small groups—in particular that the crucial evaluative decision is too exclusively rooted in the small face-to-face group. They would prefer more work in larger groups (as, for example, when Elbow treats the Teaching Practicum as one large portfolio group for the fifteen or so new TAs each fall who are teaching in the program for the first time). This complaint stems from a justifiable nervousness that different groups will evolve different standards (and a couple of groups have gotten the reputation among teachers of being "harder" or "easier"). More pointedly, there is the fear that standards will be compromised because readers in a small group often will know who the teacher is for a particular paper and therefore may feel pressured to pass it if they know the teacher wants it passed—because the teacher is their friend or is particularly defensive or edgy. (We both know from experience with the system that it hurts when your own student's portfolio is failed and you think it deserves to pass: you are deeply involved with this student and gratified by his or her enormous progress.)

These are serious worries raised by conscientious teachers, and we feel them ourselves—though the majority prefers the emphasis on small groups. (In fact we suggested having a larger group this last time and only five volunteered.) Did we start off giving too much autonomy to small groups because of our strong predilection for giving teachers their head and because of Stony Brook's strong tradition of total teacher autonomy? Perhaps. Anyway, we've made three policy changes this year that provide somewhat greater commonality or corporate functioning to the portfolio system:

(1) We now have large meetings in the middle and at the end of the semester to read sample papers or portfolios. All teachers must attend. We agree on, or negotiate verdicts for, sample papers or portfolios. The change helps keep standards more consistent since formerly we left this calibrating function to individual groups.

(2) We are now instituting a programwide response sheet to attach to all failing dry run papers and all failing portfolios. These forms will present, as it were, a common voice of the program to augment the more local voice of the reader or small group and will have checkable boxes that represent programwide categories as to weaknesses in portfolio papers—though of course individual readers will also write a short comment in a space provided. (We have seen occasional comments that were *too* cryptic or idiosyncratic.)

(3) Portfolios may now be revised if they fail with only one weak paper. The old policy increased pressure on readers not to fail an unsatisfactory portfolio if it somehow seemed clear from internal evidence or from special pleading from the teacher that the student was really quite skilled and diligent and should not have to repeat the course. Our new policy makes it easier to stick by tough standards—to say, "This isn't good enough"—but still give students a chance to redeem themselves. (This rewrite policy represents a compromise between those who wanted to allow *all* failing portfolios to be revised and those who wanted to stick with our original no-rewrite policy.)

In effect, these additions of programwide consistency are designed to save our emphasis on small collaborative groups for evaluating writing proficiency. Perhaps in the end we will conclude we should jettison that emphasis altogether and use an evaluative mechanism that is more "pure" or ETS-like—less messy. But we would find that sad.

For one thing, we want these small groups to have a prominent place in our program so they can function in other ways too—not just for portfolio business. We encourage groups to form around an interest in a particular technique or approach to teaching, even to do a bit of research. We think teachers need small groups to discuss other teaching matters and for just plain gossip and support. Most teachers like them.

As for impurity in evaluation, we could take a kind of amateur "aw shucks" line and say that we don't need perfect evaluation; we care more about teaching than about evaluation; we're satisfied that this evaluation is much more consistent than the grading of individual teachers and so we don't worry that it is less consistent than some God- or machinelike objectivity. But our reading and talking with others in the field of evaluation and our experiments over more than three years tempt us to take a more uppity line. We suspect that this "impure" process may in the end represent better evaluation.

That is, on the one hand we obviously seek a kind of objectivity and quality control—we seek an evaluation process that involves outside readers with negotiated common standards. But on the other hand, because of our lively sense of the imperfections in the science of evaluating writing proficiency, we seek frankly *not* to seal off entirely the possibility of "leaks" or "pollution" into the evaluative procedure from the teacher who knows the student.

Yes, the whole portfolio system makes for messes—since it puts "objective" examiners in the same room with the student's own teacher and gets them tangled up in discussions of specific papers where the teacher may be personally involved. The system thus makes trouble. (Though in fact we've had little rancor.) But this is nothing but the trouble that results from putting out on the table what has always been in the closet in programs that evaluate with proficiency exams or leave evaluation wholly in the hands of the individual teacher. It helps to have some of these messy discussions in large meetings led by the directors of the program, but there is something to be said for letting some of them also go on in more private small groups where of course there is some impure negotiating. We think this allows for more growth in teaching in the long run.

A Different Model of Evaluation

About half the mid-semester papers fail. At the end of the semester about ten percent of the portfolios fail, but that goes down to about five percent after some are rewritten. (The number of students who must retake the course is slightly higher because a certain number of them fade away toward the end of the semester and don't complete the course—or fail for other reasons.)

We see the portfolio as a way to ask for better writing and to get more students to give it to us. By giving students a chance to be examined on their best writing—by giving them an opportunity for more help—we are also able to demand their best writing. For example in our first semester of small-scale experimenting, we discovered that when we only explained the system to students and waited till the end of the semester to evaluate (no dry run), many of them failed who obviously didn't need to fail. They hadn't put in enough time or care because they clearly hadn't understood or believed that we were requiring good writing to pass—better writing than writing exams tend to ask for, perhaps better writing than their teachers had required for a C. (We noticed an interesting difference between the experience of reading a failing proficiency exam and a failing portfolio: the failing proficiency tends to make us sad that perhaps the student "couldn't do it"; the failing portfolio tends to make us mad that the student didn't put in enough time and care.)

This sounds like raising standards and raising the passing rate at the same time. Something fishy here. But evaluation by portfolio sets aside the traditional model of evaluation or measurement (norm-referenced) that leads us to assume that grades should ideally end up distributed along a bell curve. This model of measurement aims to rank or differentiate students into as many different grades as possible, for it is a tradition of "measuring" minds; the ideal end product is a population distributed along a bell-shaped curve (as in IQ scores or SAT scores). Our portfolio process, on the other hand, builds on a different model of evaluation or measurement (criterion-referenced or mastery-based or competence-based evaluation). This more recent tradition assumes that the ideal end product is a population of students who have all finally passed because they have all been given enough time and help to do what we ask of them. (See McClelland on competence testing; also Grant et al.; also Elbow on the effects of a competence approach on teachers.)

Problems

We keep hoping that all problems can be tinkered away through further adjustments but no doubt many are inherent in the approach.

- The system makes more work for teachers. We have done all we can to keep readings from being too onerous or time-consuming: judgments are only yes/no, portfolios are judged as a single unit, cover sheets and in-class writing need not be read (usually), and comments are given only to failing portfolios—and then only brief ones. But the work remains.
- It puts more pressure on teachers and makes some feel anxious—especially those using it for the first time. If your student fails a proficiency exam, it's easy to say, "Well, I'm not teaching exam writing," but if your student fails the portfolio you are liable to feel—at first anyway—as though *you* have failed.
- Some teachers feel it dominates the course too much: as though they are having to "teach to the portfolio," as though it is too much in their minds and their students' minds, as though they are reduced to spending the whole semester on three main pieces and therefore narrowing their focus. We try to avoid this, we want an evaluation system that one can "teach to" without having to change or "pollute" one's teaching at all, a system that lets you teach almost any course.

This feeling of constraint is felt most by teachers the first time they use the system, but it is also felt by a few very experienced and competent teachers.
- Some teachers feel that our reliance on groups puts strains on their relations with other teachers in the group when they disagree over verdicts.
- Some teachers feel that the emphasis on revising—and especially the opportunity to revise some failed portfolios—babies or coddles students too much and lets lazy students get by with help and nagging from teachers and help from peers.

Strengths

But the program continues to present more advantages than problems:

- The portfolio process judges student writing in ways that better reflect the complexities of the writing process: with time for freewriting, planning, discussion with instructors and peers, revising, and copyediting. It lets students put these activities together in a way most productive for them. And it doesn't insist that students be judged on all their efforts.
- The message to students is that thinking and writing are enhanced by conversation with peers and teachers—and that first responses, although valid, need not be final ones. It also tells them that their reactions and opinions about serious matters deserve time and attention.
- It makes teachers allies of their students—allies who work with them to help them pass. Teachers become more like the coach of the team than the umpire who enforces and punishes infractions. One teacher commented, "They don't blame me for the standard they've been asked to reach. I think because of this I have a very good relationship with my students and I'm more comfortable in the role of helper than that of judge." (See Elbow, "Embracing Contraries.")
- It draws teachers together, encourages discussion about ways to help students and about standards. Inevitably, this makes standards more consistent and teachers more conscious of their teaching methods.
- It emphasizes some important complexities of audience—showing students, for example, that we usually write for more than one reader and often for readers who do not know us. Many students come to college convinced that English teachers are hopelessly idiosyncratic and rarely agree—that one teacher's rules and expectations rarely match another's. We want students to realize that teachers can agree on evaluations even if their criteria may be somewhat different. We all write for audiences of individuals who agree on some things and disagree on others—"interpretive communities." Both students and teachers need more experience and talk about this crucial issue.
- Thus the portfolio addresses a critical, professionwide problem in evaluation that most teaching sweeps under the rug. That is, to grade a paper is to interpret and evaluate a text, yet our profession now

lacks (if it ever possessed) a firm theoretical disciplinewide basis for adjudicating between different interpretations or evaluations of a text. No wonder we are uneasy in our grading. In this situation, the only source of at least some trustworthiness in grading comes from the kind of negotiation in a community that the portfolio procedure sets up. Such negotiation of a text helps teachers make connections between the teaching of writing and the study of literature.

Experiments with the Placement Exam

It was interesting for us, without special training in evaluation and testing, to find a proficiency exam in place, to go to meetings of the National Network on Testing and read its newsletter (and other material on testing), and gradually to conclude that no one really had the answer about the evaluation of writing. This realization was empowering and gave us courage to experiment.

Having done so with the portfolio and lived to tell the tale (so far, anyway), we are now experimenting with the placement exam that all students take on entrance to the university. Instead of giving students two hours for one essay as we have done in the past, we are now asking for four writing tasks: (1) twenty minutes of exploratory writing or freewriting about an extended quotation; (2) a one-sentence summary of the quotation; (3) a one-hour essay on the topic of the quotation; (4) twenty minutes of informal, retrospective process writing about the writing the student has already done on the exam.

We find this approach serves the two goals of testing that we're also trying to serve with the portfolio process. First, it improves trustworthiness of evaluation, since the readers can base their judgment on more than one piece in more than one mode. Second, it sends the message we want to send to students about the richness and multiplicity of writing as a process.

In the end we see the portfolio system as a way to try to serve two contrary but desirable goals. On the one hand, we want some programwide commonality, not only in the evaluation of proficiency but also in getting teachers to work together under some common guidelines. On the other hand, we want to provide as much autonomy as possible to individual teachers and small groups of teachers.

19. University of Maryland, College Park Freshman Writing Program

1. **Department responsible for the writing program:** English

2. **Staffing**

Percentage of freshman composition courses taught by part-time faculty members	0%
Percentage taught by graduate students	95%
Percentage taught by full-time instructors	0%
Percentage taught by assistant, associate, and full professors	5%
Percentage taught by full-time members of departments other than English	0%

3. **Enrollment policy**

Maximum enrollment	20
Minimum enrollment	15
Average enrollment	20

4. **Program size**

   Number of students enrolled in the freshman composition program

fall 1983	2,700
spring 1984	2,700

   Number of sections of freshman composition offered

fall 1983	145
spring 1984	145

History and Design

The Freshman Writing Program at College Park has changed both systematically and dramatically since 1972, when the program was directed by a graduate student, based primarily on reading and writing about literature, and attacked by the faculty senate for serving the interests of the English department rather than the interests of the university. At that time the university threatened to remove the course from the English department to the speech department. In 1973 the English department chair, Shirley Kenny, hired Robert Coogan, an associate professor interested in classical rhetoric, to direct freshman English, and the changes began.

Coogan, consulting with Edward Corbett of Ohio State University, instituted a new curriculum based on Aristotelian rhetoric: a genuine rhetorical situation was envisioned for each paper, techniques of invention were conscientiously taught, paper assignments were drawn from the rhetorical modes, and the most popular textbook was Jacqueline Berke's *Twenty Questions for the Writer*. Staff training was instituted in several areas. Prospective teaching assistants began to come to College Park one week before school in September for an orientation week emphasizing principles of rhetoric, response to students' papers, teaching strategies, and the teachers' own writing. New teaching assistants were also required to take during their first semester a graduate course called Approaches to College Composition.

Most important, the new teaching assistants were assigned in groups of four to a "master teacher," an experienced teaching assistant chosen by interview to meet weekly with a group of new teachers and to assist them in their first semester's teaching. Master teachers are released from two courses during the year to compensate them for their service. This system allows for close supervision and yet frees the director or assistant director from constant oversight. It encourages plurality of views and fruitful discussion of teaching theories and practices among master teachers, and then in turn among the teaching assistants. The master teacher system also gives new teachers the guidance of teachers not far from their first experience of facing students not naturally eager to take a required course in writing. By 1976 the master teachers had developed a staff handbook, which included recommended assignments, sample assignment sheets, teaching methods, grading techniques, and moral support.

Shortly after arriving, Coogan also took several steps to make our teaching more sensitive to the individual needs of the students. He sought, and received in 1974, money for a small Writing Center (at first six tutors, now fourteen, who see fifteen hundred students each semester); he created a new course, English 101X, for foreign students who still had trouble with grammar and sentence structure; and he created a distinct course, English 101A, for native students who (judging from TSWE scores below 33, reinforced by a writing sample) still had trouble with grammar and sentence structure. Both these courses were deliberately made parallel with, not preparatory to, the regular 101 course. Coogan's thinking was that preparatory courses are so discouraging to morale that they are less likely to foster learning, whereas students offered the challenge of achieving more than their regular 101 counterparts (and given dedicated teachers who have fewer students to work with) often meet the challenge and succeed. To ensure that students who completed 101, 101A, and 101X had at least roughly comparable skills when they finished, Coogan instituted a coursewide proficiency exam (a written exam), which students can attempt up to three times (if necessary) during the semester. If students pass their course but not the proficiency exam, they receive a course grade of Incomplete until they pass the proficiency exam during a succeeding semester.

Course Description

Since 1978, when I became director, the changes in our program have been not structural but curricular. We have benefited immeasurably from the excellent books and articles on the theory and the practice of composition teaching that appeared during the 1970s: Janet Emig's *The Composing Processes of Twelfth Graders*, William Zinsser's *On Writing Well*, Mina Shaughnessy's *Errors and Expectations*, William Irmscher's *Teaching Expository Writing*, Pat Taylor's article "Teaching Creativity in Argumentation," Joan Bolker's article "Reflections on Reading Student Writing," Mike Rose's article on writer's block, Gene Stanford's collection of teaching ideas, *How to Handle the Paper Load*, and of course many others.

As a result of our reading and experience we have demoted the rhetorical modes from ends in themselves to means to an end; we have introduced workshop peer reviews for every paper before its due date; we do not assign personal-experience papers or argumentative papers on general issues; we use no handbooks other than Strunk and White's brief *Elements of Style;* we use very few readers; we expect research (into persons, places, books, magazines, or records) for every paper. We consider the basic writing skills to be research, observation, selection, planning, writing, and revising. We encourage all students to evaluate their own writing and that of others for tone of voice, use of facts and inferences, and consideration for the reader (roughly Aristotle's ethos, logos, and pathos). We try to make students conscious of their own writing processes and to encourage them to compare their strategies with others that might be more productive. We value lively, humane writing. Our most popular textbook is now William Zinsser's *On Writing Well*. Students write six three-to-four-page papers during their semester, along with numerous exercises in skills such as finding telling facts, drawing inferences, organizing raw material, and manipulating sentence structure. Assignments include place descriptions, practical proposals, interviews, historical research papers, and studies of films, newspapers, and magazines. All students learn how to use the library, but we don't assign long research papers: shorter, more frequent writing assignments seem to teach writing more efficiently.

While our primary aim is to develop the research and communication skills of all our students, we also recognize our responsibility to ensure literacy. Most students don't need an extensive grammar review, and we teach the grammar they do need by reproducing examples of the errors that they have made in their own papers. For students who do need grammatical instruction, we use as our principal means sentence-building exercises: given a subject and a verb, students are asked, progressively, to add modifiers, phrases, clauses, participles—whatever we want to teach. What students aren't able to come up with themselves, they thus hear from their classmates, and they learn better from their classmates than they do from us, especially in an area like grammar that they are embarrassed to be still learning.

Besides what we've learned from others, we have one or two points of emphasis that we find run counter to most current practice and that we believe to be very important. First, we try to get our students to keep in mind as they write not an audience (which they are inclined to look down on) but some imagined single reader as intelligent as themselves. Second, we try to place the same emphasis on quality of evidence and quality of thought (with correspondingly less emphasis on style) that we find in the world outside English departments. Third, we try to shift as much of the responsibility for learning as we can to the students (i.e., we don't allow passive class attendance, late papers, or revisions of a paper for a higher grade). Last, and most important, we reject the seemingly universal textbook method of starting a paper with a subject or a thesis or a given form. All our papers begin with an investigation of facts. From those facts the students draw inferences and then combine those inferences to arrive at theses or at least coherent senses of direction. Papers written about literature have traditionally followed this procedure, but most other assignments in contemporary readers and rhetorics start with either a subject (e.g., automobiles) or a form (e.g., comparison-contrast). With the subject-form albatross around our collective necks, much of our improved understanding of invention, revision, and effective writing processes remains futile, because if we follow the subject→development of the form→subject→ development model of the writing process, we are still teaching students to write in a manner that is rarely practiced outside school. Closely connected with our concern that students become skilled selectors of facts is our respect for Ken Macrorie's emphasis on "telling facts" in *Telling Writing*. A writer's principal duty and principal challenge is to find facts that convey a message to a reader. This is not an easy task, but when it is accomplished, it makes matters like transitions and sentence length fade in comparative importance.

We emphasize techniques in our courses: finding the best evidence, organizing chaos, writing correct sentences, throwing out excess verbiage, punctuating with care, recognizing the effects of ethos, logos, and pathos in one's own work and the work of others. Students come to us to learn a skill, and they won't learn it if they don't practice techniques. But we sustain our interest in teaching these techniques because we believe that a writing course so taught will have attendant humanistic benefits. Students will increase their powers of seeing things from other readers' points of view; will be freed, with well-chosen assignments, from their historical and provincial limits; will overcome their dependence on conventional interpretations of experience; will have the means to combat or evade propaganda, whether from advertising, government, or their professors; will develop a sensitivity to language and to its relation with reality; and will become more self-sufficient thinkers and writers.

Program Strengths and Weaknesses

The greatest strength of our program is the opportunity it offers teachers to learn from one another and from published work about teaching composition. When policy decisions (curriculum, assignments, textbooks) are set from the top, a program can only change in leaps, bounds, and jerks. At the other extreme, when teachers are left undirected, the best information about teaching never gets into most of their hands. We find that our master teacher system, which gives us not one but six or seven not-too-different standards at any given time, gives coherence to our program and standards to our new teachers yet allows and invites teachers to grow after their first semester. A review of journal research in the graduate course in teaching writing gives our new teachers sources for new ideas, and then they trade those ideas in their offices and through the two visits to their colleagues' classes they are required to make each semester. Each spring most of our staff participates in a review of new textbooks from which we make up a (nonbinding) recommended list, but the value of that review is not so much in the list as in the opportunity to look carefully at a new book or two. Every two or three years the staff is also required to write syllabus rationales (an idea we got from the Michigan State entry in Jasper Neel's *Options for the Teaching of English: Freshman Composition*) and those rationales are placed in a widely used file in the freshman English office. Our teachers often use them too when they are applying for jobs.

There are aspects of our program that we are not proud of. First, we require teaching assistants to teach two twenty-student courses each semester: that is more work than most people can perform with enthusiasm and still sustain interest in graduate school for more than two or three years. Second, more regular faculty members should be teaching the freshman writing course. Because we rely almost exclusively on graduate students to teach the freshman writing course, too much of our staff turns over each year (almost thirty teachers out of ninety), and students with a first-semester teacher inevitably suffer through some of their teacher's growing pains. One-third of the students is too many to go through that experience. Students are still more inclined to say, in their evaluations of a freshman writing class, "I'm sure glad I got this section instead of my roommate's," than they are to write, "I expected this class to be good and it was." If more regular faculty members taught the course, and if we could draw teaching assistants from a wider pool than just the English department, perhaps some of this turnover could be reduced. Third, the current market for full-time jobs, particularly in community colleges where much composition teaching is done, is almost nonexistent (at least in this geographical area). Therefore, most of our graduate students have no obvious teaching career to turn to when they finish an MA or part of a PhD. This is a tragic waste that could be avoided by greater flexibility in state-mandated certification procedures for junior high and high school teachers. Our best PhD students, with well-written dissertations either in rhetoric or in literature, find tenure-track college jobs, and many graduate students leave either after their MA degree or later to take jobs as editors, reporters, or technical writers. But for those who like teaching, our strict institutional separation of college teachers from high school teachers has left them—especially at the MA level—at a dead end: they can't compete for college jobs, and they are not certified to teach high school. Thus, teaching-assistant morale—strongly influenced by uncertainty about the future—remains our most fundamental problem. If we're convinced that we're developing excellent teachers of composition, we ought to do better at allowing those teachers to practice the profession they have learned.

Of course there has to be some competition for positions. We shouldn't expect to place all our graduate-student teachers in the jobs of their dreams. Realistically, graduate students must expect to teach in a school considerably less prestigious than the school that they are attending, because their school hires teachers from more prestigious schools yet. But there should be some process by which a sequence of choices could be made. If not a state university, a state college; if not a state college, a community college; if not a community college, a high school; if not a high school, a junior high school. Our society unfortunately grants lower prestige to teachers who teach students at the most crucial student ages, but happily the personal rewards of teaching are unrelated to the artificial prestige of an institution. Job candidates are often surprised that they like the atmosphere so much at a school where they almost didn't want to interview. We should now be negotiating with colleges of education and state certification boards to help get more of our MA teacher-students directly into high school and junior high school classrooms.

Charles Moran

20. University of Massachusetts, Amherst
University Writing Program

1. Department responsible for the writing program: English

2. Staffing

Percentage of freshman composition courses taught by part-time faculty members	0%
Percentage taught by graduate students	90%
Percentage taught by full-time instructors	0%
Percentage taught by assistant, associate, and full professors	8%
Percentage taught by full-time members of departments other than English	2%

3. Enrollment policy

Maximum enrollment	20
Minimum enrollment	15
Average enrollment	19

4. Program size

Number of students enrolled in the freshman composition program
- fall 1983   2,200
- spring 1984   2,000

Number of sections of freshman composition offered
- fall 1983   115
- spring 1984   105

Administrative Background

The University Writing Program at the University of Massachusetts, Amherst, was created by the university's faculty senate in spring 1982. The program is an aspect of the Department of English. It receives funding from the dean of the Faculty of Humanities and Fine Arts. Its director, a professor of English, administers the program under the watchful eye of the University Writing Committee, a campuswide committee charged with the design, supervision, and evaluation of the program. The program administers all aspects of the new university writing requirement, which has two components: a freshman-year requirement and a junior-year requirement. Students satisfy the junior-year requirement by completing a three-credit writing program designed, offered, and staffed by academic departments specifically for their own majors. Students satisfy the freshman requirement by successfully completing English 112, College Writing.

Writing Program Placement Test

Students enter the freshman component of the Writing Program through the program's placement test. On the basis of their performance on this test, they are given initial placement in English 111 or English 112 or are exempted from the freshman course, without credit. Students placed in English 111 subsequently take English 112. Neither English 111 nor English 112 may be taken pass/fail. In the past two years, approximately ten percent of the entering freshmen have placed into English 111, and roughly eight percent have been exempted from English 112. Unless exempted, all students must fulfill the freshman writing requirement during their freshman year. Those who do not may have to take equivalent courses at other institutions, at their own expense.

The placement test itself is straightforward. Given a topic designed by the program staff, students are asked to write an essay. They are given one hour to make notes or outlines, write the essay, and revise and proofread their work. The students' essays are read and scored holistically, using procedures similar to those employed by many Massachusetts high schools in evaluating the state-mandated writing-competence tests. The readers, all teaching assistants in the program, are trained in the holistic scoring procedure before the reading begins and are frequently checked and recalibrated during the scoring sessions to ensure that consensus is maintained and that judgments are consistent and reliable. An important part of the training is the establishment of criteria for the evaluation of the essays. Criteria are topic-related: that is, the criteria that apply to essays written on one topic may be somewhat different from the criteria that apply to essays written on a second topic. Using the established criteria, readers rate the essays on a scale of 1 to 6. Two readers read and score each essay; if the scores differ by more than one point, the essay is given a third reading.

Course Descriptions

Both English 111 and English 112 are governed by the same assumptions: that writing is more usefully considered an activity than a subject, that a writer learns by writing and by receiving feedback on the performance, that freshman writers need to become more aware of their own writing processes, and that the primary text of a writing course should be the students' own writing. In both courses students are required to purchase E. P. J. Corbett's *Little English Handbook* as a reference work. We make no strong brief for this particular handbook. Given the existence of the junior-year writing requirement and the consequent involvement of the university faculty in the teaching of writing, we need a common reference work, and Corbett's book satisfies that need. New teaching assistants are required to use Dawe's *One to One* as a text for their first semester, and students are encouraged, not required, to look over

Peter Elbow's *Writing with Power*. But with these exceptions, the course does not use a textbook. Students are charged a lab fee to cover the cost of copying their essays, a necessary step if these essays are to be brought into the classroom in any substantial way. Instructors are permitted to bring short readings into the curriculum, but these readings may serve only as stimulus to the students' writing, which must remain at the center of the course at all times. We doubt the efficacy of the prose-models approach. We know that our freshmen have read more than they have written and that prose models, insofar as they do produce effects, will have done so by the time our students arrive at the university. In addition, time spent reading is subtracted from time spent writing, receiving feedback, and rewriting, the primary business of these courses. Both English 111 and English 112 are, in effect, studio courses, in which students perform an activity under the supervision of a practitioner who has more experience in this activity than they do.

English 111 (Basic Writing) is a conference-centered course designed for students who have real difficulty in writing rapidly, fully, and accurately enough to survive in their academic work. The course meets for five class hours each week, two more class hours than English 112 and the general run of humanities courses. We assume that students who have been placed in English 111 need more contact time with the teacher-editor than do students in English 112. During the semester the students write in class under the teacher's supervision and outside of class on their own. They work at their own pace through a sequence of generic assignments in descriptive, narrative, and expository modes, using a five-step writing process that emphasizes pre-writing and revision. We understand that writers work in radically different ways. Nevertheless, we introduce the 111 students to a five-step process that gives them some structured approach to what may be otherwise a bewildering and frightening task. We ask them to proceed in these five steps: (1) choose a subject; (2) make a list of specific details, facts, arguments; (3) organize the list by putting some of the items in categories; (4) write a first draft; and (5) revise, using the instructor's comments as a guide. This sequence of steps should make clear our debt to Roger Garrison and Donald Murray.

Before moving on from one step to another, students must confer with their instructor. Class time is thus spent in short, individual conferences, a format that enables instructors to gauge each student's progress and to direct comments to each student writer individually. Because writers are handled this way, the teacher may ignore or modify the five-step writing process when this process becomes too cumbersome or inappropriate. The object of the sequence of topics and of the five-step process is to get writers started on engaging and fruitful writing projects. That is the end of the course; assignments and procedures are a means to that end. In addition to their in-class writing, students maintain a journal, write weekly short essays, and do assigned exercises that address specific needs.

English 112 (College Writing) meets for three class hours each week. The primary activity in the course is the composition, critiquing, revision, and publication of seven essays. At the end of week one, the mid-process draft of the first essay is submitted; at the end of week two, this essay is submitted in finished form, and the second is begun. The mid-process draft of the second essay is due at the end of week three; at the end of week four this essay is turned in, and the cycle begins again. Mid-process drafts are reviewed by peers and instructors. Attached to the final draft must be all rough work, all drafts, and all peer-editing sheets. When the essays are turned in, the instructor takes the final drafts, designs a cover sheet, and takes the resulting volume to the university's copy centers, where it is copied, collated, and stapled for distribution within the class. These published essays become the text for in-class work in the following weeks.

During two of the semester's fourteen weeks, classes are suspended and all students have a mandatory thirty-minute tutorial with their instructors. The principal agendas for the tutorial include diagnosis of writing problems, editing of particular essays, review of the work that has been completed, projection of future work, and review of the journal. The tutorials are usually scheduled in the fourth and eighth weeks.

In addition to the steady cycle of published essays, students do frequent short writings, both in and out of class, as assigned by the instructor. This work is designed both to expand the writers' sense of what an essay might be and to give the students practice and direction in handling high-level abstract thought. Under this heading we include speculative writing, problem-solving exercises, and work in defining, in discovering and articulating assumptions, and in establishing—and working with—criteria. It is the program's belief that most students coming to the university can handle descriptive and narrative writing, particularly of the autobiographical kind. The students have more difficulty, however, in working with abstractions. These short writing assignments give them instruction in this activity, which is so central to the academic enterprise. Teachers are trained in this aspect of the course by Charles Kay Smith, author of *Styles and Structures,* one of the first modern textbooks to stress invention.

English 112 does not have a prescribed sequence of assignments, nor does it prescribe a sequence of "kinds" or forms. It does require students to work in a range of forms. Instead of proceeding deductively, imposing a structure on the activity, we try to proceed inductively, moving from the activity toward a structure. If a student, for example, begins the semester with a comparison-contrast essay on the differences and similarities between high school and college, our instructors accept this essay and, if it is well done, say that the student has now mastered this form, that it is time to move on to another form. We want to help students become aware of genre and able to work easily in a range of genres. As the semester goes on and the student's portfolio accumulates, instructors make it clear that one criterion used in evaluating the portfolio is the range of genres to be found in it.

Teacher Training

Because the program is staffed primarily by teaching assistants, teacher training is an absolutely critical aspect of its operation. Graduate students remain with the university for three or four years, on the average. Each fall, therefore, we begin with twenty to twenty-five teachers who are new to the program and, many of them, new to teaching. For new teaching assistants, the training program begins early in the summer, when they receive the program's *Handbook,* a booklet describing the placement-testing program, a sample syllabus, two suggested activities for the first class, and one book: Stephen and Susan Judy's *An Introduction to the Teaching of Writing*. In late August the new teachers come to the campus for a two-day workshop on the teaching of writing, during which they write, consider their experience as writers, read student writing with an eye to potential commentary and evaluation, and learn about the administrative detail that accompanies the teaching. During this workshop they are introduced to their mentors, veteran teaching assistants who are assigned to them as guides and official friends for the first semester. New teachers are required to come to biweekly workshops on topics such as conferencing, peer editing, commenting on student writing, evaluation, and invention.

Teaching assistants new and old are assigned to course directors, all tenured members of the university's English department. Each of the eight course directors has a team of eight or nine teaching assistants. The team meets regularly during the semester in short, practical seminars, and the course director visits each teaching assistant's class at least once. The course directors have two rather different roles: they are master teachers, a resource for their younger colleagues; and they are evaluators, quality-control personnel who monitor the teaching assistants' performance in the classroom. The course directors all teach one section of Basic or College Writing, and they receive a one-course reduction in their teaching load to compensate them for their teacher-training and supervisory work.

Teacher-training activity is coordinated through the Writing Program Resource Center, which is staffed by one of the program's assistant directors and four veteran teaching assistants. The Resource Center maintains a library of books and articles on the teaching of writing and a library of teacher-training videotapes that focus on activities such as introducing a class to peer editing, opening a conference, and teaching the writer's voice. Through the Resource Center each new teaching assistant is videotaped twice during the first year of teaching. Resource Center personnel help the new teacher read and interpret the videotape.

Strengths and Weaknesses

The freshman program is just now completing its second full year. It has been well received by students, who rate the courses highly on their annual teacher/course evaluation forms. The teachers also seem happy with it. Most students feel that they have become better and more confident writers, and most teachers feel that they have seen their students grow substantially as writers. It seems clear to this writer, at least, that the program's focus on the activity of writing has been justified by the results.

The weaknesses of the program are a function of its strength. To concentrate so absolutely on the activity of writing, even for a single semester, brings us face to face with the complexity of the rhetorical situation that is characteristic of most academic writing. Who are our students writing for, and why? Our students seem less bothered by this problem than we are. We do use peers as audience, and we do publish the essays for the classes. But the teacher lurks behind the peer, and why does the teacher want to read? Outside the academy the writer can easily discover audience, voice, and purpose. Inside the academy the situation is substantially artificial and much less clear, particularly in a non- or pandisciplinary freshman course. In the junior-year courses this problem can be less acute. The physics major can write review essays, the major in nursing can write family reports, and the English major can write literary criticism. A freshman writing course, because it catches students before they have elected a major, finds itself in this single respect somewhat at sea. One can help writers understand the activity they are learning to perform, but in a world that is at some distance from authentic discourse.

21. University of Michigan, Ann Arbor
English Composition Board

1. **Department responsible for the writing program:** English Composition Board

2. **Staffing**

Percentage of freshman composition courses taught by part-time faculty members	0%
Percentage taught by graduate students	90%
Percentage taught by full-time instructors	10%
Percentage taught by assistant, associate, and full professors	0%
Percentage taught by full-time members of departments other than English	0%

3. **Enrollment policy**

Maximum enrollment	NA
Minimum enrollment	NA
Average enrollment	22

4. **Program size**

    Number of students enrolled in the freshman composition program

fall 1983	1,893
spring 1984	1,300

    Number of sections of freshman composition offered

fall 1983	98
spring 1984	80

On 16 January 1978, the faculty of the College of Literature, Science, and the Arts at the University of Michigan overwhelmingly approved the following proposal for an English Composition Board and a new composition requirement:

The Board

A. The English Composition Board shall be composed of six faculty members, two from the Department of English and four from other departments or programs within the College. One member of the Board from the Department of English shall be the department chairman.

B. The Board shall be an agent of the College faculty, responsible to every unit in the College but the responsibility of none. Its budget shall be provided by the Dean and its chairman appointed by the Dean for a three-year term. The chairman's work for the ECB shall be considered half of his or her teaching responsibility.

C. The Board shall be responsible for offering immediate intensive instruction in English composition to all students who may present themselves or may be recommended by their instructors as needful of special help.

D. The Board's tutorial work shall be accomplished by both faculty members and Graduate Student Teaching Assistants (GSTAs) who have special interest and competence in teaching English composition. The ECB shall pay an appropriate portion of the salaries of both its faculty members and GSTAs; the Board shall supervise and train where necessary the GSTAs who teach for it.

E. The Board shall provide assistance and guidance in the transaction of teaching composition to faculty members or GSTAs who may request such help in planning or offering courses which carry with them potential credit or certification in English composition. The Board shall accept responsibility from the College Curriculum Committee for approving the writing component of such courses offered by any unit in the College.

The Requirement

A. All students entering the College for the first time must compose an essay before registering for their classes. According to competence demonstrated in this writing sample, students shall be placed in one of three categories:

1. *Tutorial*: A two-to-four credit tutorial, offered by the ECB, which must be taken in the first semester after matriculation; the tutorial course precedes the Introductory Composition course taught in the Department of English.

2. *Introductory Composition*: A four-credit course, taught in the Department of English, which must be taken in one of the first two semesters after matriculation.

3. *Exempted*: No introductory composition requirement to fulfill before the upper-level writing course or program.

B. A writing course or program must be completed by all students, usually in their area of concentration, after their sophomore year.

As the English Composition Board implemented the new writing requirement, it assumed responsibility for developing and administering two types of activities that were requested by the faculty but were not part of the writing requirement: a Writing Workshop to provide the support of experienced composition teachers to all undergraduate students in the college at any stage of a writing task, and a program of in-service seminars and conferences on theory and practice in the teaching of writing for teachers of preuniversity students who might enroll in the University of Michigan.

When the Michigan faculty voted for an English Composition Board and a new writing requirement for the College of Literature, Science, and the Arts, not only did it invest a unit apart from the Department of English with overseeing the college's writing program, it also stipulated that the majority of board members come from departments other than English, thereby ensuring the cross-curricular character of the instructional program. Furthermore, faculty members in all disciplines assumed responsibility for teaching the argument and organization of writing in their respective disciplines to juniors and seniors. They built into the program their expectations that junior and senior students would be prepared to learn the argument and organization of writing in the disciplines in introductory composition courses.

In effect the ECB took shape as a seven-part program, with six parts within the college and one beyond its confines. The board's six responsibilities within the college are the administration of an entrance essay, required of all incoming undergraduates; tutorial instruction required of all students whose entrance essays indicate a need for such assistance; introductory composition, required of most students to make them more proficient writers; writing workshop support, available to every student; junior- and senior-level writing courses, offered and required primarily in students' areas of concentration; and research into the effectiveness of all parts of the program.

School-College Cooperation

The seventh part of the program was designed to include five activities relating the teaching of writing in secondary schools and community colleges to the writing program at the university: writing conferences, intended primarily to inform preuniversity teachers of the ECB's program of instruction and of its ability and willingness to engage in outreach projects; one-day and two-day seminars conducted in secondary schools, community colleges, and universities throughout the state of Michigan and beyond, designed to familiarize faculties with the college's writing program and to discuss with teachers current theory and practice in the art of teaching writing at all levels; writing workshops, held at the University of Michigan, designed to provide teachers with three days of intensive work in the teaching of writing; extended curriculum and staff-development projects undertaken as models with a few school districts that requested such service; and publication from 1979 to 1983 of *fforum*, a journal providing teachers of writing with a meeting place for mutual instruction and dialogue. This seventh—outreach—part of Michigan's writing program has effectively provided the board a vehicle for informing preuniversity teachers in Michigan and beyond of the writing competence students will need to succeed in the college's writing program.

Placement Exams

All students who enter the college write placement essays for one hour during their orientation visit to the university. These essays not only require students to demonstrate mastery of writing competencies that the faculty values but also signal the importance that the college places on writing. The essay prompts require students to copy into their bluebooks two initial sentences, which determine the topic, tone, style, and thesis for an argument about an issue with which they are likely to be familiar. Students are evaluated for their ability to sustain the position they choose to argue as well as for their ability to communicate in the register and type of writing dictated by the assessment prompts.

Two experienced composition teachers—faculty members who have undergone extensive training in holistic reading—evaluate each essay according to criteria determined both by faculty expectations of student writing and by student essays examined during experimental administration of the writing assessment. If two readers fail to agree on the quality of the essay, a third reader resolves the disagreement. Depending on the evaluation of their essays, students are placed into either tutorial classes or Introductory Composition or are exempted from taking an entrance-level writing course.

Course Descriptions

Those students whose writing skills will not serve them effectively in the college are required to enroll in tutorial writing classes. In these classes a maximum of sixteen students receive concentrated instruction in writing from experienced, full-time composition teachers. Tutorial classes meet for four hours each week, and students in those classes meet individually with their teachers for at least one half hour a week. At the end of seven weeks, those tutorial students who demonstrate sufficient growth as writers in a posttest essay move on to an introductory composition course or are exempt from any further introductory-level instruction; those who continue to require tutorial instruction must enroll in another tutorial section.

Students may fulfill the introductory composition requirement by completing one of several courses. Most students elect to take English 125, Introductory Composition, taught in the Department of English primarily by graduate-student teaching assistants. This course is designed to give students experience in writing for a variety of audiences, purposes, and situations in a wide range of content areas. Students may also fulfill the requirement by completing English 167, Shakespeare, also taught in the Department of English; Great Books, taught within the Great Books department; College Thinking, taught as one of the university courses and administered by the office of the academic vice-president; or a freshman seminar taught in the residential college by faculty members in a variety of areas and based in any substance the instructors choose.

After they complete the introductory composition requirement, all students must take one of the upper-level writing courses taught by professorial members of the departments, who are usually assisted by TAs funded and trained by the ECB. In each of these upper-division courses whose substance is its subject matter, writing functions as a primary vehicle for learning and communication.

Writing Workshop

Supporting every aspect of the college's writing program is the Writing Workshop. Heavy use of the Writing Workshop indicates that it provides significant support to student writers throughout their undergraduate work in the college. During a typical academic year the Writing Workshop is open for more than sixteen hundred hours.

> [In 1980–81] 1,157 students made 1,909 visits to the Workshop (or 1.65 times per student); if only those students making more than one visit are counted, the average number of multiple visits is 3 per student, supporting the claim that the Writing Workshop is an important center for sustained instruction in writing. Many of the students who visit the Workshop are former tutorial students who seek additional help from familiar faculty. In 1980–81, however, about one-third of the visits were made by juniors and seniors who, in virtually all cases, had no prior experience with the ECB but learned of the help available at the Workshop through faculty referrals, posters and advertising, or word-of-mouth from others who had been helped. (Bailey 12–13)

Conclusion

The English Composition Board has conceived broadly its charge from the college to develop and implement a new composition requirement, and it has placed its introductory composition courses firmly at the center of a program for writing that begins in students' elementary schools and continues thoughout their formal education. Implicit in Michigan's writing program are the following assumptions and messages: introductory composition is a misleading rubric for any writing course—even the ones it labels as such; a course of study in composition must recognize that all individuals are always composers, and, informed by this recognition, instructional programs must be designed; introductory courses in writing must be embedded in students' previous instruction in writing, and they must look forward to composing tasks that students will subsequently be asked to fulfill; providing students with instruction and practice in writing must be the work of all teachers, all the time; to do this work well, teachers of writing at all levels must engage continually in conversations about the demands for reading and writing that both the academy and society place on students and citizens.

Dorothy G. Grimes

22. University of Montevallo
University Writing Program

1. **Department responsible for the writing program:** English

2. **Staffing**

Percentage of freshman composition courses taught by part-time faculty members	20%
Percentage taught by graduate students	0%
Percentage taught by full-time instructors	0%
Percentage taught by assistant, associate, and full professors	80%
Percentage taught by full-time members of departments other than English	0%

3. **Enrollment policy**

Maximum enrollment	24
Minimum enrollment	NA
Average enrollment	22.5

4. **Program size**

Number of students enrolled in the freshman composition program

fall 1983	624
spring 1984	501

Number of sections of freshman composition offered

fall 1983	28
spring 1984	22

History

The structure of the entire writing program at the University of Montevallo grew out of a three-year study of the core curriculum undertaken in 1980 on the recommendation of the academic vice-president. The focus of the study was much broader than just writing; it included the entire set of general education requirements. However, it soon became obvious that structuring a writing component of a core curriculum is different from structuring a course entity. Supported by an administration committed to improving instruction, the Core Curriculum Committee and the English department set out to shape a writing program responsive to the larger needs of the university—both the need for coherence in the freshman year (sometimes referred to as the horizontal dimension of writing across the curriculum) and the need for consistent reinforcement of writing ability in the other three undergraduate years (the vertical dimension).

Freshman Course Descriptions

The freshman courses that resulted from the study—two three-semester-hour courses titled Foundations in Writing—unify the curricular and co-curricular experiences of the freshman year and, at the same time, introduce students to academic discourse. As a unifying center, the courses are coordinated with two other courses taken in the freshman year, Introduction to the University Experience and Foundations in Oral Communication. Introduction to the University Experience

> introduces UM students to the nature of the University, to the special responsibilities it assumes in our culture, and the opportunities it offers.... [It] helps insure that UM students understand that the University experience includes setting goals; articulating problems; exploring personal, collaborative, and institutional resources; developing strategies; and understanding modes of inquiry in the disciplines.

The link between Foundations in Writing and Foundations in Oral Communication is intended to restore the long-lost connection between speaking and writing. As an introduction to academic discourse, the freshman courses help students become accustomed to using writing as a means of learning, of coming to terms with reading in the various disciplines through writing summaries, syntheses, and reflective papers as well as through writing personal responses to their academic experiences.

General Assumptions

Influenced by the Beaver College model developed by Elaine Maimon, who directed a 1982 NEH Institute on Writing in the Humanities in which three Montevallo faculty members participated, the writing program is based on the following general assumptions about writing:

1. A written discourse reflects a complex set of recursive processes, processes closely connected to those of thinking, reading, speaking, and listening. Although all the aspects of these processes may not necessarily be analyzable, writing can be taught (in the context of reading, speaking, and listening) as a way of both discovering and communicating meaning.
2. Since most public writing begins with some form of private writing, writing instruction should recognize the value of private writing and encourage students to develop a habit of using writing to reflect on their own experiences.
3. Purpose and audience are the primary shaping factors in discourse. Thus writing instruction should recognize the need to help students

discover their aim, find their own voice, and imagine their audience.
4. Because academic writing within the various disciplines is the product of what Elaine Maimon, Kenneth Bruffee, Joseph Williams, and others have called socialization within a community, writing instruction should provide opportunities for students to learn to work within an academic community and to form judgments about their work and the work of others.
5. Although writing is often described as a skill, it cannot be meaningfully taught in isolation from a body of knowledge. The written products of a discipline reflect the modes of inquiry, the kinds of knowledge, and the methods of communication characteristic of that discipline. Introductory writing courses, therefore, should acquaint students with the writing of representative disciplines. Similarly, courses in the various disciplines should include instruction in the writing of those disciplines.

The description of the Foundations in Writing courses reflects the assumptions outlined above:

> An introduction to college writing, these courses present writing both as a means of learning and as a means of communicating what one learns. They enable students to understand the writing process, including the demands of purpose, audience, and occasion; they give them experiences with writing tasks that are common to all academic writing; they enable them to produce the kinds of writing appropriate for the context; and they help them read and respond to their writing and to the work of other writers in a constructive way. In addition, they acquaint them with the conventions of writing in a variety of disciplines so that they might more readily handle writing assignments in other classes, preparation for which is one of their stated objectives. Finally, they help the students become confident about using the conventions of Standard Written English.

The goals of the freshman writing program (approved by the English department in 1984) show more specifically the aims of introductory writing courses:

1. To help students use writing as a tool of liberal learning, particularly as a means of understanding what they read, of thinking critically, and of clarifying values;
2. To help students understand their own writing process and thus to gain confidence as writers;
3. To help students value to a greater degree their personal writing—writing as a means of reflection, a mode of creativity, a source of pleasure;
4. To help students understand the interrelatedness of reading, speaking, listening, and writing;
5. To help students to follow an argument and to present their own thoughts in an orderly and intelligible way;
6. To help students become proficient in handling the structures of the written language;

7. To help students use responses from their instructors and their peers to revise their work in progress, and to help them learn to read and respond to their classmates' work in progress in a constructive way;
8. To help students analyze and write for the needs of different audiences and, in particular, to introduce students to the modes of discourse among the various academic disciplines within the university community;
9. To encourage students to use the library as a resource for learning;
10. To make students aware of the importance of observing the conventions of grammar and mechanics.

When the English department approved these goals, it also approved an honors track of Foundations in Writing, available to students with ACT scores in English of 27 and above, as well as a one-semester course, Preparatory English, recommended for students with ACT scores in English of 14 and below. Preparatory English does not count toward the student's Foundations in Writing requirements, although it does carry credit as a university elective. These courses were officially implemented in September 1985. Texts for the regular Foundations in Writing courses are *Reading, Writing, and Reasoning* (Sternglass), *The Confident Writer* (Gefvert), *Writing in the Arts and Sciences* (Maimon et al.), and either *Readings in the Arts and Sciences* (Maimon et al.) or *The Conscious Reader* (Shrodes et al.). Instructors may choose to use a sentence-combining text in addition to the required texts.

One of the assumptions of the UM writing program is evident in the title of the freshman courses, Foundations in Writing. The title presupposes reinforcement. Much of this reinforcement is done informally throughout the curriculum. A list of "Desired Characteristics of General Education Courses" disseminated by the General Education Committee makes writing seem almost essential in general education courses. According to that document, general education courses should "provide opportunities for active modes of learning; provide opportunities for students to develop higher cognitive skills such as problem solving, analysis, synthesis, interpretation, and evaluation; provide opportunities for students to develop skills in writing, speaking, listening, and computing, especially as these skills also develop the higher cognitive skills listed above; and promote the integration of knowledge and an understanding of the interrelationship of knowledge, skills, and attitudes."

Writing Reinforcement Courses

Yet a university made up of some 2,500 students in four colleges needs a more direct, intensive way of reinforcing writing ability throughout the four years. The revised core, therefore, sets up a series of writing reinforcement distribution requirements:

> These courses, designed by faculty members from any discipline in the University, reinforce the writing ability that the students acquired in the Foundations in Writing courses. Thus they are the central means of extending writing practice

through the four years of the students' college experience. Six hours of Writing Reinforcement courses will be taken during the sophomore year, three in the junior year, and three in the senior year. The inclusion of these courses in the core will add no additional hours to the requirements for most students, since some general education courses and some courses required for the major and minor in each department will be approved by the University Writing Committee and the General Education Committee for designation as Writing Reinforcement courses.

The implementation and monitoring of the overall university writing program (with the exception of Foundations in Writing) is handled by the University Writing Committee, an eleven-member faculty committee made up of representatives from the four colleges. To help provide the consistency essential to a comprehensive writing program, the University Writing Committee established the following criteria for writing reinforcement courses:

1. Courses are to be made available for sophomores, juniors, and seniors. Those for juniors and seniors are to be designed primarily for majors and minors. Six hours of Writing Reinforcement courses will be taken during the sophomore year, three hours in the junior year, and three hours in the senior year.
2. Writing requirements in Writing Reinforcement courses are to be integral to course content and course credit.
3. Through the use of multiple drafts, writing as a process is to receive as much emphasis as does the final product. Thus student revision based on responses from the teacher, and possibly from other students by means of a peer review, should be incorporated in the process of helping the student to develop a more logical, organized, professional style and product.
4. In most instances, multiple shorter writing assignments should be used rather than single lengthy term papers. For example, a sequence of several assignments might be devised so that these lead to a final product characteristic of writing in that discipline. Since writing encourages a student to become an active rather than a passive learner, short but frequent ungraded writing assignments should also be included. These might take the form of journal entries, summaries of class lectures, or responses to reading assignments.
5. It is recommended that enrollment in a course section be limited to 25–30 students.

Two valuable models for the committee's work on these criteria were similar documents from the West Chester State University and the University of South Alabama.

There is some evidence that student writing improves even without specific instruction when students are explicitly told that writing is an important part of a course. On the basis of such evidence, the university has no doubt made progress toward improving student writing, for faculty approval of this rather ambitious program surely contained that explicit message. In its initial stages, the writing program has attempted to make the most of the effects of expecting better writing. The English department distributed desk copies of the freshman English handbook to every university faculty member.

The accompanying letter pointed out that "the fact that we value good writing can be communicated to students by something as simple as a textbook on our desks." In 1982, the English department also initiated the President's Awards for Excellence in Writing. The awards of $100 each are given in three categories—freshman English, sophomore English, and all 200- to 400-level classes throughout the university. The entries must be essays resulting from an assignment in a class. Teachers may select one essay from each of their classes for submission.

Faculty Development

Our experience also suggests that, similarly, writing instruction improves when faculty members realize that it is an important part of their job. Just as faculty approval of the writing component of the core curriculum has made students aware that writing is to be more important than before in disciplines other than English, approval of the writing component made the University Writing Committee keenly aware of the need to help instructors in the disciplines become confident in using writing to teach subject matter. To meet that need, the university funded a series of workshops for thirty faculty members in spring 1985. Attendance at these workshops was required of those who planned to submit a course for approval as a writing reinforcement course. (The series will be repeated in fall 1985 and 1986 for other faculty members.) Participants were paid stipends of $250 for five days—three immediately before the beginning of the semester (January) and two immediately following spring graduation (May). In addition, participants were asked to attend three half-day sessions during the semester.

Although some faculty members initially opposed the University Writing Committee's decision to require the workshops, most participants came to realize that the workshops were essential. Sequencing the workshops throughout the semester made this group of participants instrumental in the shaping of the writing program itself. It gave the participants and the Writing Committee a sense of discovering together the implications of the guidelines for the program already set by the Writing Committee. Some degree of receptiveness to the concept of using writing as a mode of learning had already been established by earlier workshops with voluntary attendance from across the campus.

The difference between these earlier workshops and the required ones in spring 1984 was not the quality of the consultants but rather the local context into which the workshops fit. The participants saw the required series as directly meeting already established curricular and pedagogical needs. Thus our program seems to demonstrate two of the functions that writing workshops can serve: (1) to establish a climate receptive to curricular and/or pedagogical change and (2) to help faculty members become more knowledgeable and confident about teaching writing in order to meet already established curricular requirements.

The three-day workshop in January (conducted by Carol Holder, director of Writing in the Disciplines at California Polytechnic University at Pomona) concentrated on designing assignments and evaluating writing. The use of the guidebook *Improving Student Writing*, coauthored by Andrew Moss and Carol

Holder, gave participants a textbook to consult throughout the semester. The three half-day sessions dealt with such topics as connections between the freshman writing course and writing reinforcement courses and gave participants an opportunity to review their colleagues' assignments and work out questions about assigning and grading writing. The two-day May workshop (conducted by John Bean, director of writing at Montana State) focused on using writing to enhance cognitive growth. Participants were encouraged to think not only about connections between the freshman writing course and writing reinforcement courses but also about connections between writing reinforcement courses at the various levels beyond the freshman year. An introduction to Piaget and Perry naturally leads to the question of what kind of growth in writing one can expect in the undergraduate years. When participants began to grapple seriously with this question, it was clear that they had claimed the writing program as their own.

Conclusion

In short, our writing program is a work in progress, and those of us at the center of it hope it will always be regarded as such. From the present vantage point, we can see things that might have been done differently, but probably few of us would, in fact, do them differently if we had the opportunity. In the first place, we are aware that in revising writing programs, as in most curricular changes, one gains efficiency by not attempting to involve the entire faculty in the initial stages of learning and planning, but one loses a degree of involvement and ownership that would make the program move more quickly and smoothly later. We deliberately chose, primarily because administrative support was readily apparent, efficiency over involvement.

Second, putting a curricular structure into place does not guarantee genuine change. Genuine change takes place only as individual faculty members discover that writing can bring active learning into their classrooms. Furthermore, the writing reinforcement courses could even work against a broadly based writing-across-the-curriculum program. Unless most faculty members are committed to teaching writing reinforcement courses and to using writing as a means of promoting active learning, the writing reinforcement courses can become, like the English department, the dumping ground for complaints about student writing. Likewise, from the student's point of view, writing reinforcement courses can become mere legalistic requirements—quantitative obstacles to graduation. Our program deliberately aims at higher literacy, not at minimum competency, and if writing reinforcement courses should come to be regarded as such traps, the program would not have accomplished its purpose. Thus one remaining goal of the University Writing Committee is to design a long-range plan for evaluating the program as it is officially implemented.

Our program has attempted to build on the best experiences of other university writing programs, adapting to fit the needs of our own university community. Our program is closely tied to our core curriculum revision. Writing reinforcement courses are, in fact, the only component of the general education program that extends through all of the student's undergraduate years. Our faculty's current commitment to making the revision in general education work is one of the reasons our program has been successful so far.

Gary H. Lindberg

23. University of New Hampshire Freshman Composition Program

1. **Department responsible for the writing program: English**

2. **Staffing**

Percentage of freshman composition courses taught by part-time faculty members	0%
Percentage taught by graduate students	63%
Percentage taught by full-time instructors	28%
Percentage taught by assistant, associate, and full professors	9%
Percentage taught by full-time members of departments other than English	0%

3. **Enrollment policy**

Maximum enrollment	26
Minimum enrollment	NA
Average enrollment	26

4. **Program size**

   Number of students enrolled in the freshman composition program
fall 1983	1,100
spring 1984	1,175

   Number of sections of freshman composition offered
fall 1983	43
spring 1984	46

History and Design

The core of the present UNH freshman English program was established when Don Murray directed the program in the early seventies after publishing *A Writer Teaches Writing*. The staff at that time began to explore the concept of writing as a process and discovered that the instructor could be far more helpful during that process than at its end. In their efforts to give the writer more and more control, autonomy, and reponsibility in that process, the instructors experimented with two techniques that have become essential to our course: the weekly or biweekly conference between the instructor and the individual writer and the workshop in which peer writers read, discuss, and edit one another's work. Both techniques placed a whole new emphasis on writing as revision. And both placed the initiative—even in responses—with the writer instead of the critic. In reaction to the earlier practice of teaching freshman English as a literature course, the staff duplicated the students' own writings for workshop analysis and depended primarily on them as course readings. Freshman English became a *writing* course.

Later some assigned readings were reintroduced to give students practice with reading and interpretive skills and to stretch their awareness of alternative writing modes, but the emphasis has remained on writing and revision. We do not use a textbook as the pattern of the course, and we do not have a set sequence of writing assignments for all sections. Individual instructors design their own courses within certain broad guidelines and share their successes and failures in weekly staff meetings. All students turn in five pages of writing per week, sometimes as a single paper, sometimes as a shorter paper and an assigned exercise or reading response, sometimes as a thorough revision of an earlier paper. In a typical section approximately one-third of the class time is spent with each of three activities: in-class exercises to practice various thinking skills and writing modes, workshops on student papers, discussion and written interpretation of assigned readings. Each instructor designs the sequence of exercises and workshop approaches for his or her own section and chooses the readings to assign. By varying the specific emphases in workshops and reading discussions, instructors try to guide their students' practice through a range of diagnostic and interpretive strategies.

All students write a research paper, but we do not otherwise require particular kinds of writing of every student. We emphasize the writer's own discovery of subjects and of ways to make something of those subjects, and we urge each student to try a range of writing modes. But we are less concerned with taking students through an abstracted set of writing lessons than with working on writing *in context*. The strength of both the weekly conferences and the peer workshops is that they help students to understand principles within their immediate practice and at the same time to see how various writing qualities actually come together and complicate one another in a real piece of writing. Repetition with a variation of emphasis better describes our approach than does any step-by-step sequence for writers. We regard writing and learning to write as recursive activities. The essence of our program is guided practice. Instead of giving students lessons or lectures or textbook chapters, we provide the occasions for them to practice making meaning, not only in the writing of their own essays but in critiquing and editing their peers' work, in exercising specific writing strategies, and in building interpretations of assigned readings. Even in conferences we try to have the writer take the lead in assessing the strengths and the problems in the essay.

Because of the structure of our program, we do not track students in freshman English. A very few students are exempted by the Advanced Placement Test, but almost all our students take the course. We do not have remedial sections. The conferences allow us to tailor the course to each writer's own strengths and weaknesses, and we find that the differences in previous skills and experiences among our students are potentially an advantage in the peer workshops, for students bring a genuine variety of perspectives to one another's papers, and we encourage them to respect that variety and to learn from one another.

Theoretical Assumptions

We place what I think is an unusual amount of responsibility and trust on our individual teachers, letting them design their own sections within broad guidelines. Our assumption is that as long as we share certain basic principles and a theoretical knowledge of various heuristic strategies, the actual course design and teaching methods are best invented and adapted by the teacher who is going to work with them. Here is the teaching philosophy of our program as I wrote it up for the guidance of our new teaching assistants.

Teaching Freshman English

If there is a philosophical core to the freshman English program at UNH, it is that we treat our students as writers and our staff as teachers. There is no subject matter the students are being led through, no knowledge they must absorb. Instead, we want them to experience what writing is all about: those moments when feeling finds form, when experience discovers language, when ideas come together and spark new ones, when the interests of the writer cross over to the expectations of readers. Only the individual writer can make those moments happen. There is no formula. Nor is there a curriculum for instructors, a set pattern for the course. We want them to experience what teaching is all about: the immediate occasions when general principles actually inform our handling of particular problems, when the teacher's personal interests find a way of reaching to the student's personal needs, when the lesson does not come from the textbook but grows out of the occasion and illuminates it. Only the individual teacher can make such moments work, and only by bringing to them knowledge, imagination, and attentive eyes and ears. What makes good writers and good teachers is not following rules or models but finding form. The act of finding and forming is the soul of both writing and teaching—it is at the center of our program.

This does not mean that anything goes, for either writer or teacher. Making things up as one proceeds is not finding form. Just as writers need to know the range of choices open to them, the various strategies by which they can make meaning, so teachers need to know about various ways of structuring courses, alternative writing strategies to share with their students, various formats for what can happen in class. Students learn less from a preset lesson on complex sentence structure, for example, than from a teacher's ability, when a student actually uses a complicated structure, to seize on the occasion in order to explore its possibilities with the class. In other words, teachers should know grammar, forms of writing and thinking, possibilities of course organization, ways of conducting a class. This knowledge informs the actual choices that bring both a course and a class session into being and adapt it to the needs of the students.

Teachers in freshman English develop this kind of knowledge in several ways. They read books on the teaching of writing before they begin, and there is a library of textbooks and resources in the composition office that the staff uses regularly. The required course on the teaching of writing examines both practical problems and alternative theories of composition. In weekly meetings of the freshman English staff, we hear presentations by experienced teachers, do workshops on teaching strategies, discuss particular problems in the course, and explore ways of leading students into new kinds of thinking. And finally individual teachers constantly share their experiences, problems, and solutions with one another.

What works for one teacher or one writer may not, of course, work for another, and that is why we don't prescribe models or course designs. When we exchange exercises or classroom methods with each other, we don't look at them as the right ways to teach or as engaging ways to use up a class hour. Instead, we look at them as examples of personal solutions. We examine the exercise for what writing principles it develops, what it does to the relation between teacher and student, what it does to relations among students in the course, what place it has in a larger context. This kind of scrutiny—which applies also to textbooks we scan—allows us to adapt other people's insights to our own situation and needs.

The staff itself is a community of teachers in the same sense that the individual class is a community of writers and readers. In both cases, respect for individuality is essential—it is what allows us to share. We build on one another's insights, listen for what kind of truth the other person has found, use it to help us reflect on our own procedures and values. Even experienced teachers of composition constantly change and develop their approaches. Just as good writers use a workshop of peer readers less for praise than for solutions to the problems they are having, so freshman English teachers look for help from one another. We find by such sharing that no teaching problem is unprecedented, but at the same time each problem as it occurs has a twist of its own.

What makes both kinds of communities actually work is good faith. Teachers have to believe that they can make a difference. Writers have to believe that they are writers, that they have said something, that it matters. One of the most important things we do as teachers is to make sure our students as writers have reason to experience that belief—to give them occasions when they can produce writing that matters, to recognize as their readers when they have done something special, to create a classroom atmosphere in which writers respond honestly and precisely to what has worked in another's writing and to what hasn't worked. The classroom is sustained by the same kind of mutual faith as sustains the staff itself—I have to believe that you have something valuable to say, some experience from which I can learn.

Staff and Training

The majority of our composition staff members are graduate teaching assistants. Those in the MA programs have two-year assistantships, those in the doctoral program, five years; in a given year, therefore, a little less than half our teaching assistants are new. We also hire approximately a dozen composition instructors each year who teach two courses each semester and who each supervise the work of one incoming teaching assistant. Most of these instructors are our own graduated students who were especially effective as classroom teachers and who have shown a continuing theoretical interest as well in the teaching of writing. All beginning TAs take a course on the teaching of composition, and many go on to take one of the seminars in composition that allow them to carry on research. Approximately half of our MA students are enrolled in one of the graduate writing programs (fiction, nonfiction, or poetry), and their experience of graduate workshops and conferences reinforces their own use of these techniques in teaching freshman English. All of our staff members regard themselves as both writers and teachers, and they often share their own writing experiences with their students. The majority of our graduate students have as lively an intellectual interest in their teaching as in their own graduate work, and the result in staff meetings is very free and energetic discussion on both practical and theoretical matters. At least half a dozen members of the full-time English department have central interests in the teaching of composition, and the rest of the department shows strong support for the program.

Strengths and Weaknesses

The greatest strength of our program is in the morale and engagement of the staff. Because they are given autonomy and responsibility in a supportive atmosphere, they bring a great deal of thought, energy, and imagination to their teaching. They are not teaching someone else's method or syllabus or lesson. Even when they are still getting their initial classroom experience, their energy and personal commitment win respect from their students. In a similar manner, our program puts the emphasis for students on learning their own autonomy and responsibility and confidence as writers. They gain real facility at finding good subjects, making something of them, and exploring the possibilities of revision.

Because of the emphasis on student writing and on free choice of topics, there is a risk in our program that students will explore only a narrow range of writing modes and that they will not try really demanding strategies of thought. Similarly, the staff, without a structured sequence of lessons and assignments, risks not covering enough ground. We are trying to avoid these dangers in two ways. First, we are spending more time with assigned readings in which students have to cope with a real range of thinking skills and have to do some writing as part of the very act of reading and interpretation. Second, we are trying through staff meetings and workshops to keep our staff aware of the various heuristic strategies and acts of mind that student writers should encounter and practice.

Given the structure of our program, we simply cannot know that all our students will have "had" everything we might guarantee by running them through a large textbook. But that uncertainty is more than offset by the kind of experience that both students and teachers have through the development of their own autonomy. They find themselves immersed in a process for which there are no foolproof rules or formulas, and they learn to draw on their own resources and to collaborate as well in coping with that process.

Paul J. Kameen

24. University of Pittsburgh Composition Program

1. **Department responsible for the writing program: English**

2. **Staffing**

Percentage of freshman composition courses taught by part-time faculty members	45%
Percentage taught by graduate students	45%
Percentage taught by full-time instructors	0%
Percentage taught by assistant, associate, and full professors	10%
Percentage taught by full-time members of departments other than English	0%

3. **Enrollment policy**

Maximum enrollment	22
Minimum enrollment	8
Average enrollment	20

4. **Program size**

    Number of students enrolled in the freshman composition program
fall 1983	2,400
spring 1984	2,400

    Number of sections of freshman composition offered
fall 1983	125
spring 1984	120

Assumptions

The composition program at Pitt has been shaped from the outset by a coherent vision that now informs its entire curriculum. The basic assumptions about the nature and purpose of composing are as follows:

1. Composing involves not simply the mastery of a set of strategies for shaping received knowledge. It is defined and taught as a method for becoming more knowledgeable, for putting together texts that bear the original stamp of individual thinking. While composition is an academic discipline in its own right, at the same time it is not the sole property or responsibility of any one department. Composing is intrinsic to all disciplines, and the English department has been instrumental in shaping the recent curricular reform, which calls for a genuine writing requirement across the curriculum.

2. Composing is a literary activity and not simply a process of structuring content into forms. Students are expected not only to write competently but also to develop worthwhile things to say. Thus, composition and literature, reading and writing, remain always companionable in their most essential aspects. In this respect, composition retains its vital links to the context of English studies, out of which it has been emerging as an increasingly significant scholarly field.

Undergraduate Curriculum

The undergraduate curriculum is composed of about ten separate courses, a variety of testing mechanisms, and the Writing Workshop. Before Pitt students begin the freshman year, they are tested in a variety of different ways—including a monitored writing sample—to determine which composition class they are best suited for. The majority find themselves in General Writing, which is now a required course in the context of the new curriculum (see Appendix).

A variety of features distinguish the General Writing course from more traditional freshman writing courses. The most salient is the amount of writing it demands: students write between fifteen and twenty complete essays. But more important is the emphasis on sequencing in the assignments they are responding to. By focusing on a single subject, like "teaching and learning" or "reading and writing," the students are being asked to explore from various angles what they have to say, to write in the same way that real writers write: by shaping their thoughts into language and by allowing language to reshape their previous thoughts.

In producing their own texts, students are also producing the primary text for the course. Many class periods are spent discussing copies of student papers to examine critically the language that students choose to think with. The Pitt approach grounds its pedagogy not in any prescribed rules for composing but in a rigorous discussion with and among students about their own writing.

Another significant area of the undergraduate curriculum is Basic Writing. Pitt has for years been at the forefront of a national movement to redeem basic writing from the stigma of remediation, which leads most such courses to be little more than a series of exercises and drills in the proprieties of grammar and punctuation. At Pitt, the Basic Writing courses are methodologically identical to General Writing. Students are asked from the outset to write complete essays, to read and question one another's work, to learn to write by writing. Students learn how to see the patterns of error that characterize their work; they learn to revise the structures that support them. Like all the university's composition students, they learn writing as a way of knowing.

The basic writing curriculum also includes Basic Reading and Writing, a six-hour course developed over the last few years in response to a need to provide another mode of instruction for students with extremely low language proficiency, students who were not being adequately served by Basic Writing. These freshman courses are supplemented by an array of advanced or more specialized courses and, more importantly, by the tutorial services of the workshop, one of the first of its kind at a major university. Employing the equivalent of five full-time faculty lines, the workshop provides over two thousand tutorial hours to about six hundred students every semester. These clients range from freshmen with basic problems to graduate students preparing dissertations. The workshop also serves as a training facility for students from the School of Education and as an arena for research, providing resources for both faculty and graduate students to design and execute experimental studies. This sort of activity is likely to increase as computer facilities become more accessible and more sophisticated.

Graduate Curriculum

Because the Pitt approach emphasizes pedagogy, the graduate area in composition has always been closely affiliated with the undergraduate program. Pitt requires a rigorous, two-semester graduate seminar in the theory and pedagogy of composition, which student instructors take in concert with teaching their own sections of General Writing. Like the students they teach, graduate students are asked to read and think and write about writing—to compose for themselves both a theory and a pedagogy of composition. The graduate curriculum also includes a Seminar in Basic Writing, available to advanced graduate students who simultaneously teach Basic Writing, and a range of optional courses in rhetorical theory and methods.

What distinguishes the program from many others is that graduate study in composition is intimately related to graduate study in literature and literary theory. The connection between reading and writing that informs the undergraduate curriculum is even more pronounced at the graduate level. Composition is an optional area of specialization under the more general heading of a PhD in literature. And the courses in composition theory are designed to mesh with rather than compete against course work in the central literary aspects of the discipline.

Pitt's programs in English have, therefore, avoided the fragmentation and alienation that afflict advanced programs elsewhere. In this respect, Pitt is at the horizon of English studies. A sizable contingent of the literature faculty teaches composition courses regularly, and such courses as Basic Reading and Writing, the Language of Science and Technology, and Literature and Ideas, have bridged entirely the traditional distinctions between composition and literature.

Appendix

The following writing requirement was initiated in fall 1983 as part of a general reform of the curriculum:

> At present Basic Writing or its equivalent is required of all entering students who are deficient in basic composition skills. This requirement went into effect in the Fall term, 1979. But the skills acquired in Basic Writing are by no means equivalent to the literacy we expect of college students and college graduates; indeed, these basic skills should have been acquired long before the student came to college. The present proposal is designed to increase the probability that our students will learn to write well while they are in our care.

1. (a) All students must successfully complete one composition course beyond Basic Writing. This course may be selected from among those courses in composition currently offered in the English department, and for which successful completion of Basic Writing or its equivalent is prerequisite; *viz.*, General Writing, Critical Writing, Writing Arguments, Research Writing, Advanced General Writing, and Written Professional Communication. As an alternative, the student may choose from among those Freshman Seminars or other courses approved for this purpose by the College Writing Board.

   (b) Students may be exempted from this requirement by achieving a sufficiently high score on the diagnostic writing test, or on the recommendation of the instructor in Basic Writing, Basic Reading and Writing, or U-CEP 22, subject to the approval of the Director of Composition, or on the basis of a special examination.
2. The College will identify courses in individual departments as W-courses. These courses will have a minimum number of writing assignments, spaced out over the term. If term papers are required, drafts should be due and available for discussion before the last month of class. Students would be expected to produce at least 20–24 pages of writing and to engage in some revision. All students will be required to pass a minimum of two W-courses at some time beyond their freshman year, or one W-course and one English composition course (in addition to any courses taken to fulfill the Composition requirement).
3. A passing grade in a W-course will constitute certification by the instructor that the student has adequate proficiency in writing for the purposes of study at that level in the College.
4. The English department will assist in the planning of W-courses or the evaluation of student writing at the instructor's request. The department will also make materials available and sponsor seminars on writing for interested faculty. The writing workshop will be available as a resource for writing problems that seem too basic or baffling to be dealt with in the normal course of instruction.
5. The College will establish a College Writing Board to oversee the implementation of the writing requirement and the approval of W-courses.
6. Freshman Seminars and W-courses may also be used to meet general education requirements if approved for that purpose.

Susan Miller

25. University of Utah
University Writing Program

1. Department responsible for the writing program: University Writing Program

2. **Staffing**

Percentage of freshman composition courses taught by part-time faculty members	12%
Percentage taught by graduate students	80%
Percentage taught by full-time instructors	0%
Percentage taught by assistant, associate, and full professors	5%
Percentage taught by full-time members of departments other than English	3%

3. **Enrollment policy**

Maximum enrollment	21
Minimum enrollment	15
Average enrollment	19

4. **Program size**

   Number of students enrolled in the freshman composition program

fall 1983	839
spring 1984	722

   Number of sections of freshman composition offered

fall 1983	33
spring 1984	40

Background

In 1981 the University of Utah began a major reevaluation of writing instruction at the freshman level and concluded, with the help of faculty members from each of the major undergraduate colleges on campus, that its one required freshman English course was inadequate on a number of grounds: First, placement into this course—or placement into a two-quarter preparatory sequence before it, or exemption from it—was based on inadequate and oversimplified standardized test scores (16 ACT). Second, traditional freshman English taught for one quarter perpetuated a remnant from historical rhetorical education for public speaking—the myth that students learn to write and read critically before the classroom and personal situations shape the purposes of their reading and writing. Third, the traditional requirement suggested that the Department of English could fully prepare students for all reading and writing they might do. And fourth, traditional exemptions from required composition reinforced the errors in each of these points while also excluding those better-prepared students who benefit most from instruction in making their own discourse.

A universitywide Task Force on Writing reported to President David Gardner and the university senate that correcting these erroneous assumptions would require using a more accurate placement essay rather than standardized scores; instructing all students in writing without exemptions based on scores, AP courses, or CLEP tests; and developing writing-intensive courses in liberal education and in disciplinary majors. The task force recommended that a sequence of eight writing experiences, two at each level of a student's career, be required. By 1984, these recommendations were translated into funding from the National Endowment for the Humanities "Excellence in a Field" education grants for the initial stages of the development of a University Writing Program. The University Writing Program is a separately budgeted program in the College of Humanities, governed by a director and a board that represents every undergraduate college, student affairs, and student government. The board is charged with monitoring and developing writing curricula, personnel actions, and course development on campus.

Course Descriptions

The University Writing Program is now the curricular home of Writing 50, 51, 101, and 110. Writing 110 is a new course, planned originally for the twenty percent of students previously exempted from composition. But the new placement essay results have revealed that previous standardized test scores were regularly misplacing (in a random pattern) twenty-five percent of the students. Writing 110, in its first year, is enrolling only about ten percent of the students entering the university. We have also found that only about three percent of entering students need two preparatory courses and—as would be expected in the homogeneous culture of Utah—that about seventy percent appropriately enter Writing 101. Since the Writing Program is currently funded only at the freshman level, its principal accomplishment to date has been to reconceive the purposes and practices in those courses. Since we have acknowledged that learning to write is a developmental process that depends on the particular contexts that stimulate, and eventually respond to, the writer's purposes, instruction at the freshman level concentrates on two aspects of public writing in educational settings: reading expository prose and learning the typical purposes of academic assignments. Students in all freshman courses write in response to readings, beginning with their own writing and with selections they choose in Preparatory Writing 50 and 51. In Writing 101 and 110, they read, write about, and imitate selections that exemplify the purposes and habits of public writing.

Freshman writing assignments stipulate contexts and genres of writing rather than patterns of organization (e.g., comparison contrast). They typically call for summaries, abstracts, essay examinations, analyses of style, imitations, or position papers. In Writing 110, students devote two weeks to stylistic analysis and write annotated bibliographies and proposals for papers rather than a long research paper. The University of Utah library offers a course in methods that students may take concurrently with either 101 or 110.

While the content of these courses appears product-centered, the methods attempt to sequence and spiral the process of writing each piece. Teaching methods focus on guiding students in prereading, workshop groups, and revision. Grades are suspended until the middle of the course, and the last portion of each course is devoted to revision and editing practice so that students are finally graded on what they have learned rather than on how well they write initially. The midterm and final in-class essays are group graded so that students and teachers focus on the classroom teacher as coach rather than evaluator.

Faculty Development

Each new freshman writing course is decidedly an experiment, and each is undergoing revision in light of the experiences of teachers and students. One outcome of the Writing Program's novelty and of NEH funding has been the luxury of full participation and responsibility on the part of graduate student teachers from English, communication, and economics and of faculty members from psychology, whose active evaluation of these courses is necessary in light of the need to report grant outcomes. Another unexpected outcome has been that the program's revisions of freshman instruction encourage faculty members in disciplinary courses to assign writing they have avoided because it has not been publicized as part of "regular freshman English." Summaries and essay examinations are becoming more common across campus, reinforcing the importance of writing to learn.

New teachers in the University Writing Program participate in a weeklong orientation before classes start and then take a two-quarter colloquium designed to emphasize three aspects of teaching: preparing for each week's assignments, focusing on particular teaching techniques, and surveying rhetorical and composition theories relevant to teaching needs. Additionally, the program has, in conjunction with the Department of English and the Women's Studies Program, received the first grant of its kind from the Western States Women's Consortium, to ensure teachers' awareness of gender issues in language and in language teaching. This project, directed by Ann Parsons (English), was implemented in 1985. Participation in all aspects of teacher training by teachers from disciplines other than English has supported the program's focus on writing as a way of learning in all disciplines.

Problems and Prospects

As in any new situation, the program's problems are those that accompany a "paradigm shift," especially one as subtle as articulating the four principles outlined above when previous models appear to accomplish the same goals. The relation between the Writing Program and the Department of English is, naturally, more complicated than abstractions or grants can clarify:

teachers attach the stress of changed curricula to the separation of the program from the department; administrative turf is claimed, reclaimed, and relinquished by both sides; faculty members are naturally skeptical about principles that replace generalized humanism with more populist epistemic rhetorics. The final resolutions of each of these loci for tensions will be broadly interesting because the University of Utah's experiment is potentially a model for multilevel cross-curricular writing instruction in public institutions across the country. As its development is now planned, the program will provide ad hoc help to all the university's departments over a three-year period so that they may establish writing-intensive courses as well as determine what continuous support from the Writing Program they need. After this period, development of a postfreshman requirement called Introduction to Discourse: Humanities/Fine Arts/Social Sciences/Science is planned as a part of the liberal education requirement. These developments depend on further funding and support from within the university. (For further information and samples of syllabi, placement criteria, or the funded grant proposal, please write to the program administrator, Sylvia Morris.)

Joan Graham

26. University of Washington Interdisciplinary Writing Program

1. Department responsible for the writing program: English

2. Staffing

Percentage of IWP courses taught by part-time faculty members	0%
Percentage taught by graduate students	40%
Percentage taught by full-time instructors	60%
Percentage taught by assistant, associate, and full professors	0%
Percentage taught by full-time members of departments other than English	0%

3. Enrollment policy

Maximum enrollment	20
Minimum enrollment	5
Average enrollment	15

4. Program size

Number of students enrolled in the IWP program
   fall 1983   200
   spring 1984   200

Number of sections IWP courses offered
   fall 1983   12
   spring 1984   12

At the University of Washington the Interdisciplinary Writing Program (IWP) links writing courses with lecture courses. The Writing Links are not merely support for lectures, for they carry an equal amount of credit and are graded independently. But writing teachers do give up some autonomy in exchange for the chance to do exceptionally rewarding work. In effect, they participate in the interpretive communities defined by lecture-course studies and work with students in the contexts where they actually need to write. Teachers gain by capitalizing on students' motivation and by focusing on tasks that invite the use of writing as a tool of inquiry. Particular purposes of inquiry are better defined in associated lecture courses than they can ever be in isolated "expository" or "persuasive" writing courses. Students in linked writing courses use writing as a means of discovering and exploring ideas, not just a means of displaying them. Distinctions between writing and thinking virtually disappear.

The IWP now offers about fifteen linked writing classes each quarter, and some features are common to all: whether a writing class is linked with a lecture in art history or in sociology, students can expect that some time will be spent examining the lecture-course textbooks as writing performances. They can also expect their own writing to be the constant subject of study in class and in small peer response groups. And they can expect individual conferences with teachers on the strengths and weaknesses in the required drafts of their essays. Beyond these basics, however, Writing Link activities vary with the purposes, methods, and values of the accompanying lecture course.

An international political economy course, for example, requires papers based on wide-ranging research. Each student chooses a country and spends the term studying ways that internal changes have been provoked or influenced by the country's interactions with other countries. Evaluating widely varying sources is an important early concern for each student, and constructing an argument—the controlling idea of a paper—requires considering theoretical perspectives from lectures as well as a mass of new information from independent reading. Probably the most common problem is getting lost in the information, all of which is at first assumed to be valuable just because it is newly gained.

Different demands create different problems for students writing history papers. Western civilization assignments often call for a particular kind of text analysis: students are asked to consider primary sources as documents revealing their place and time. What can be inferred about the society for which the *Odyssey* was written? Is there evidence in Tacitus's *Annals of Ancient Rome* that the empire in Nero's time was well governed, peaceful, and secure—despite Tacitus's own dramatically negative evaluation? Do Froissart's *Chronicles* suggest that fourteenth-century Europeans perceived themselves to be living in a time of crisis—as twentieth-century historians say they were? Or an assignment may be based on a secondary text, requiring analysis of a particular historian's treatment of a period. What's difficult is recognizing the signs of authors' perspectives and drawing appropriate inferences from what is and isn't said.

Students in all Writing Link courses work on the development of ideas. But invention activities may focus on analyzing texts in history, public events in political economy, individual behavior in psychology, ethical claims in philosophy. All linked writing classes also discuss approaches to organization and problems of clarity, but again these matters are considered in context, dramatizing the organic relations between purpose, content, and form. That we work deliberately with the tasks and values relevant to particular writing occasions should not suggest that our courses are narrowly utilitarian. We stress the importance of context not because we're concerned with discrete, locally important "skills" but because we want to cultivate students' perceptions of what writers see and do—and of the ways that purposes guide their work. For the same reason we don't present general rules or plans for "good writing"; instead we push students to generalize for themselves about the sources of good effects in their own, each other's, and professional writers' work—effects always evaluated with respect to purpose.

Writing Link activities acknowledge that students must become better readers to be better writers and that they must gain confidence in their legitimacy as makers of meaning. Many have never had their writing taken seriously, nor have they taken it seriously themselves. Discussions about the clarity, appropriateness, and sufficiency of a writer's intentions develop naturally when the subject concerns all the students, when it is relevant both to their own writing and to their lecture-course study. And the quality of observations that students can make about one another's work improves conspicuously with practice. We press for specific sources of good effects, for possible alternatives when problems are identified, and at all times for attention to signs that suggest why problems occur and where writers' intentions are incompletely realized. As teachers we comment this way ourselves, so even though we will be grading students' finished work, they perceive us more as advocates than as judges of their thoughts.

Faculty Development

Because a linked writing course promotes students' active learning of new material, most lecturers welcome the arrangement. Their obligations are not greatly increased—they need only meet a few times with the writing instructor to settle calendar questions and talk over the design and intention of writing assignments. It would be common for a lecture course to require two essays during a quarter, and those would also become part of the assignment pattern in the Writing Link. In addition, the writing instructor would probably seek the lecturer's advice on the assignment of two more essays to be used in the Writing Link only but designed to draw on lectures and required readings. The calendar for each linked writing course, including due dates for drafts and final versions of essays, is coordinated with that of the accompanying lecture.

The amount of interaction between lecturing faculty and writing faculty varies with individuals' interests and available time, but there is always some, and the mutually stimulating effects are often great. Writing instructors are not expert in lecturers' fields, but they are attentive listeners and readers and experienced writers, so they voice their questions about the intentions of writing assignments—and that frequently leads to clearer articulation of assignments and richer development of possibilities. The effects go beyond the Writing Link classes themselves, since most of these classes are optional companions to large lectures: many students who are not taking a linked writing class will nevertheless be required to address the lecture-course writing assignments. The enrollment in most lecture courses accompanied by Writing Links is between one hundred and five hundred students; with a given lecture there may be two Writing Link classes, limited to twenty students each. The students who take both lecture and writing courses benefit by doing two-thirds of their quarter's work in coordinated classes; but the students who take only the lecture benefit from the presence of the writing class too. Besides encouraging fuller statements of joint assignments, writing instructors often alert lecturers to students' preparation problems. That may lead to lecture-course discussion of analytic methods, perhaps to the explanation of problems and potentialities in a sample of student writing for the benefit of the whole lecture group. Many lecture groups are broken into discussion sections led by teaching assistants once or twice a week. Writing instructors participate in lecturers' meetings with TAs and may bring openings from students' essay drafts or offer ideas for short pieces that can be written and discussed in the sections. Taking up opportunities to expand and improve the general use of writing in instruction is an informal aspect of Writing Link teachers' work.

Faculty development values come the other way too. Writing teachers attend the lecture classes and read course textbooks as well as other professional writing in the lecture fields. By studying discourses of disciplines and of lecture classroom communities, they further their theoretical understanding of the relations between language and thought. One immediate, practical result of the fact that they are not professionals in a discipline is that writing teachers become conscious of unspoken intellectual frameworks, which they can help students recognize and exploit as opportunities. Their teaching environment is exceptionally stimulating, and they are constantly studying what they find in both student and professional work.

Curriculum

A full teaching load in the IWP is two classes a quarter. That means teachers will usually be attending two different lecture courses, often in different disciplines, in order to make full use of students' shared experience in their own courses. Most of our Writing Links accompany lecture courses in social science disciplines, including anthropology, political science, sociology, history, international studies, psychology, and economics. Humanities bases for Writing Links include art history and philosophy, and, beginning in the winter of 1985, two natural science courses in our general curriculum became the bases for new links. We also offer every fall several Writing Links in conjunction with honors-program core lectures in the natural sciences, social sciences, and humanities. Although these lectures are limited to forty students, two Writing Links accompany each core course because they are a required part of the honors program and are taken by nearly all the students.

It is because Writing Links are optional when they accompany lectures in the general curriculum that those lectures have to be large: typically, ten to fifteen percent of the students taking a lecture will also enroll in a Writing Link. Demand for spaces in a given writing class varies somewhat with the importance of writing in the associated lecture, but the necessary block scheduling for linked courses always inhibits some enrollment. In addition, most students don't initially understand just what such courses are. Some students are attracted to them immediately, often the especially scared who need help to survive, and the especially ambitious and strong. Demand has increased enough that the IWP now offers twice as many classes as it did four years ago. But an innovation of this kind is sufficiently fundamental that time must be allowed for changing student expectations about writing courses—what they can do, where they'll be found, what arrangements they require.

Possibilities and Problems

Brief experiments with linked courses have been made in various schools in the past, usually inspired by two teachers who recognized that by helping each other they could help themselves. But expansion from a single course to a program has happened only rarely. Sometimes simply announcing the availability of a linked course was deemed sufficient, and students ignored the offering; sometimes scheduling problems were not solved; sometimes registration information was not well timed or well publicized; sometimes a successful linked episode seemed so uniquely the creation of two particular teachers that its promise as an example went unexplored. Linked-course program development does take energy and patience. It depends, in part, on cultivating among students and also among faculty members an improved understanding of the functions that writing instruction can serve. Link courses undercut the tendency to associate writing instruction with remediation, so once begun they help smooth the way for more of their kind. By stressing engagement in demanding tasks, they keep the focus on what student writers have to say and so address in a motivating context all levels of problems and possibilities. It is because linked courses are both so practical and so intellectually challenging that they are worth the work.

That conclusion is unanimous among the twenty teachers who have been on the staff of the IWP over the past seven years. Teachers in the linked-course program at the University of California, Davis, are similarly convinced, as are those in a third program at UCLA. Davis now offers about the same number of linked writing courses as the UW and lists them as special sections of English composition. The UW's program developed as an independent unit in the College of Arts and Sciences, and its courses were initially listed under General and Interdisciplinary Studies. But visibility of such listings was low—students who want to find writing courses usually look under English. A recent administrative change is certain to have some effect: the IWP is now an activity of the Department of English and its courses are listed as such.

The level at which linked courses are offered, and their relation to writing requirements, must also be considered in developing a program design. UCLA's linked courses accompany upper-division lectures for majors, while the UW's courses are lower-division general education features, with about two-thirds freshman enrollment. The UW has done a few experiments with upper-division lecture links, and they were fully successful. But upper-division lecture groups are smaller, so the pool of students is usually insufficient as a base for an optional writing link. Also, there is a strong argument for offering freshman courses that stress writing to learn. Administrative practicalities and priorities may determine the level at which linked writing courses are offered, but there is no apparent limit on instructionally valuable contexts.

The UW has little experience with the effect of general writing requirements on a linked-course program, because such requirements are only now being reestablished. We do, however, have the directly relevant honors pattern referred to above: honors students fulfill their writing requirement by enrolling in writing courses linked with core course lectures. A school might establish a similar pattern for students in the general curriculum. If each freshman took a linked writing course with one of, say, five large general education lectures, each lecture might have seven or eight linked writing classes. A considerable number of classes might then be staffed by TAs—so long as each set included some professionally invested, experienced faculty, and the sets of teachers met regularly and frequently to discuss their work. At the UW the maximum is two Writing Links with a given lecture; fewer then forty percent of our linked classes are taught by TAs, who, as less experienced teachers, are always assigned to one of the links in a set.

The complete IWP staff is now five full-time postdoctoral faculty members and six half-time predoctoral teaching assistants. We need at least that proportion of faculty because we do so much course innovation and because we maintain links with lectures in so many disciplines. Every full-time faculty member has a strong theoretical interest in language use, as do three half-time staff members who are completing their graduate studies in English. The other three half-time staff members are graduate students in history, political science, and sociology—disciplines with which linked courses have been offered longest. Chosen for their special interest in effective teaching, these TAs often help train junior TAs in their home disciplines.

The IWP was created as a way of breaking down barriers between disciplines that inhibit language study and cripple teaching. The identification of subjects with disciplines and departments in academe has separated writing as a subject of study and instruction from reasons for writing, insofar as those reasons are not primarily aesthetic. Linking courses is one way of crossing departmental lines. Furthermore, linking courses makes it possible to respect an insight regarding language use that increasingly prevails in literary studies: that language inevitably embodies community assumptions about what is significant and what it means to know.

We believe that crossing departmental lines to put writing instruction in context is indisputably valuable. But crossing those lines is not easy when curricula and reward structures are departmentally defined. The development of the IWP was aided by the Fund for the Improvement of Postsecondary Education. After we had done a first experiment with the linked-course design in 1975, and nine more experiments by 1977, FIPSE made us a two-year grant that regularized a pattern of offerings. A series of severe budget cuts at the UW then inhibited expansion for a while, but the IWP is now a growing, increasingly influential enterprise. It participates with five other schools in the NEH-supported Pacific Northwest Writing Consortium, but its basic activities are entirely funded by the university.

The program's success is based on the fundamental assumption that learning is recognizing and articulating relationships. Students and teachers value linked writing courses not only for their intellectual rigor but for their integrative effects. When students write about what they study, observations on their writing are generative, not alienating. Because the courses do not artificially separate content and form, they lead naturally to the advancement of thought. Students' engagement is personal, though their writing is not about their private lives. And teachers never wonder whether their efforts count.

Karen Pelz

27. Western Kentucky University
The Pilot Project

1. **Department responsible for the writing program:** English

2. **Staffing**

Percentage of freshman composition courses taught by part-time faculty members	57.7%
Percentage taught by graduate students	11.5%
Percentage taught by full-time instructors	0%
Percentage taught by assistant, associate, and full professors	27.9%
Percentage taught by full-time members of departments other than English	2.8%

3. **Enrollment policy**

Maximum enrollment	25
Minimum enrollment	15
Average enrollment	21.3

4. **Program size**

   Number of students enrolled in the freshman composition program
fall 1983	2,328
spring 1984	1,659

   Number of sections of freshman composition offered
fall 1983	104
spring 1984	75

Western Kentucky University has a two-semester sequence of freshman English courses required of all students, although some students may be exempted from English 101 or place into honors sections of English 101 and 102 on the basis of their ACT scores. Transfer students for whom English 101 and 102 are not appropriate are required to take English 301, Intermediate Composition; this course is also part of the minor in writing, which includes courses in expository, technical, business, and creative writing.

Traditional and Pilot Programs: Course Descriptions

There are currently two varieties of freshman English offered at Western: the "traditional" and the "pilot," the second being an experimental program that began two years ago. The director of freshman English is responsible for the entire freshman program, and the director of the pilot project is responsible for designing the pilot courses and providing faculty development for those faculty members who volunteer to teach in the project. At the end of its third year, the pilot project will be evaluated by a departmental committee, which will make some recommendation to the department as to what form freshman English will take in the future.

The traditional program in English 101 and 102 has existed in more or less its current form for a number of years. In English 101 the emphasis is on grammar, usage, and the common forms of expository essays: narrative, description, classification, comparison-contrast, persuasion. Typically the texts are the *Harbrace College Handbook* (Hodges and Whitten) and an essay reader. Students write from six to eight compositions, and much class time is devoted to the study of grammar and usage. About two-thirds of the way through the term, students must take an exit examination, a hundred-item multiple-choice test on mechanics, punctuation, and usage; they must pass this exam in order to pass the course (although a retest is possible at the end of the semester for those who fail the first test). In addition, students are required to read a novel, chosen from a list of about a dozen, and usually are asked to write about it.

The traditional 102 course focuses on persuasive essays and the term paper. Students must also read another novel, chosen from a second list. Typically about half the semester is spent on teaching the research paper. Students also write eight to ten persuasive or expository essays. The exit exam for this course is a one-hour essay, written in class and scored analytically, with half the scoring of the test weighted towards grammar, punctuation, and usage. The Freshman English Committee has recently recommended that this exam be given in one two-hour time slot to allow time for editing and revision (the department has voted this policy into effect) and is considering a change to holistic scoring.

I designed the pilot program in freshman English when I came to Western Kentucky University from Dartmouth College in the fall of 1982, and I serve as its director. To some extent I have to talk about what it was in its first two years and what it is now, since the experimental courses have changed. Faculty participation in the pilot project has been strictly voluntary. The first year I had eight colleagues teaching with me; in 1984, thirteen; in 1985, twenty-two. From the beginning, teaching assistants have been invited to join us, but only a few have chosen to do so. The rest of the faculty members are about equally divided between full-time and part-time teachers. For the first two years we used Gene Krupa's *Situational Writing*; those who wanted to also asked their students to purchase copies of *Harbrace*. We taught a novel from the required list, and students wrote at least one and often several essays based on the novel. In 102 we used Ken Macrorie's *Searching Writing* as our text for the "I-Search" papers, exploratory research projects on topics students have a personal interest in investigating (students wrote two, one of which had to involve the use of library sources) and a Norton Critical Edition of the instructor's choice; this novel and the critical essays in it were the basis for a sequence of essay assignments. The exit examination for English 101 Pilot is a one-hour, in-class, holistically scored essay; in 102 Pilot we had our students take the same exam as those students enrolled in the traditional sections. Given my choice, I would not use exit examinations in a writing course, but both the department chair and the director of freshman English felt we might encounter legal problems if some students had to take an exit exam and others did not, so we have exit exams in the pilot project.

In the fall of 1984 we changed textbooks in the pilot courses. Both *Situational Writing* and *Searching Writing* are excellent texts, and teachers and students alike responded positively to them, but we felt that we did not want to continue teaching from the same texts year after year. I have written a freshman composition text, *Exploratory Writing*, designed especially for the pilot project or courses like it at other universities, and we use that text in English 101. In English 102 we use either *Write to Learn* by Donald Murray or *Writing with Power* by Peter Elbow, and writing assignments are structured around a single text, such as *Walden*, or a single theme, such as coming of age, facing death, or love. We create sequences of assignments that include expressive, expository, and persuasive essays, and the research project is related to the text or theme being explored in each section. Descriptions of the material to be covered in each section are available to students before registration so that they can choose a section that interests them. We also have a new handbook to replace *Harbrace*: *A Writer's Handbook* by James Flynn and Joseph Glaser.

From the beginning the pilot courses have been based pedagogically on the research of James Britton (*The Development of Writing Abilities* 11-18). Our students generally come to us with little experience in writing beyond the occasional five-paragraph theme and a research paper or two, perhaps properly researched and documented, perhaps not. They have studied some grammar and some literature in high school but, by and large, very little writing. Most of them need, then, to begin at what Britton calls the expressive level or what others might call the personal essay, essentially narrative and descriptive in mode and based on personal experience. Such writing helps to develop fluency and a "comfort zone" in the writing class. In my text, for example, some of the expressive writing assignments include describing a place that has been home to the students, describing a person they know well, telling about a time someone tried to get them to do something they didn't want to do, telling about a time they suffered some kind of loss, speculating about what their lives might be like twenty years from now, and writing in journals.

After several initial assignments in expressive writing, we move to what I call exploratory writing, which combines elements of expressive and transactional (expository) writing. And from there we move to the other two kinds of writing James Britton describes in his book, transactional and poetic (creative). The assignments are arranged in sequences so that, for any topic being explored, the students write four pieces: expressive, exploratory, transactional, and poetic. This movement is essentially developmental in terms of thinking skills as well as writing skills; it allows the students to begin with something they know well (personal experience) and move through stages to writing about more abstract ideas or to writing more analytically. Here is an example of how one such sequence works:

- Expressive assignment: I ask the students to write about their lives in twenty years—not what they think their lives will be like, but what they want their lives to be like.
- Exploratory assignment: The students read two brief selections that have to do with nuclear energy: a passage from Jonathan Schell's *The Fate of the Earth* and a *New York Times* editorial by Noel Perrin on the Three Mile Island incident. Then I ask the students to explore what their lives might be like if they happened to live through a nuclear disaster of some kind twenty years in the future. How might such an event alter their dreams for the future?
- Transactional assignment: The students are asked to reread the Schell and Perrin material and to make a brief opinion statement about nuclear power. Then they think of all the arguments they can use to support their opinion, then all the arguments that could be mustered against it. They meet in small groups to share their notes and add to one another's arguments. Then they write a persuasive essay about some aspect of the nuclear debate.
- Poetic assignment: The students are asked to write a poem, short story, or one-act play that has something to do with the topic of nuclear disaster—perhaps a poem using some of the images in the Schell article, perhaps turning their first or second essay into a short story or a play.

There are four such sequences of assignments in the text, for a total of sixteen writing assignments. But assignments that follow this developmental pattern can be created on any subject, and when we move into English 102 in the second semester, we will again begin with expressive and exploratory assignments, as a way of getting into the subject; as the semester progresses, however, we will emphasize the writing of critical, analytical, and persuasive essays, culminating in the research project.

Again because our students are inexperienced writers, we spend a lot of our class time teaching them ways to approach the writing process: generating, structuring, adding and deleting, developing, revising, editing. All the books we use—*Exploratory Writing, Write to Learn, Writing with Power*—contain useful information and helpful advice about these various stages of the writing process, and that is a primary reason they were chosen as texts for the courses. Generating and revising are stages that most students have had little instruction in or experience with, so we concentrate on those stages. In English 101 our students write about a dozen essays and pick three of them for revision; in English 102 the students write six to eight essays and the research project and again choose three to revise.

Pilot classes are conducted as writer's workshops. All essays are originally submitted as first drafts and are not graded; only revised essays are given grades, and some instructors choose not to grade individual papers at all but rather to grade the entire portfolio of each student's writing when it is handed in, revisions included, at the end of the semester. Usually at least one class a week is a writer's workshop, where the students meet in small groups to respond to one another's papers. We have discovered through experience that students do not know what to say about papers when they first begin participating in a workshop; the instructor needs to model the response approach and to provide them with some guidance that will help them respond intelligently to each other's writing. However, once the students have developed these techniques, the small groups are of great value in giving them practice in editing and revising their writing. Often when the students are ready to write the final draft of a paper, we have special copyediting sessions in which they all search for problems with grammar, punctuation, and usage. What direct teaching of those elements we do in the pilot courses arises out of the student papers themselves; the students bring their handbooks to class on those days, and we work together to straighten out infelicities of language in the final draft stages.

Faculty Development

Faculty development is an inherent part of the pilot project. We meet for a day-long workshop the week before classes begin to talk about the theoretical and pedagogical assumptions of the course as well as to deal with practical matters, such as how to get students' papers duplicated for the workshops and what to do if your class has been scheduled for a room where the chairs are bolted to the floor. Throughout the semester we meet for an hour every week to discuss how the course is going, share problems and successes, practice working in small groups and responding to student writing, and train ourselves for the holistic scoring of the exit exam. The faculty members who have volunteered to teach in the program have been extremely cooperative and good-natured about meeting so frequently and patient about working out the bugs inevitable in any new system of doing things. Each semester we work together to collect, edit, and publish student papers from the pilot courses, and both the English department and the President's Development Fund have been generous in their support of the project.

Program Strengths and Problems

We have, of course, had our problems. There is something slightly schizophrenic about running a traditional and a pilot program side by side in any institution. Despite our attempts at communication, there is always confusion at registration as to whether that course with the P after it is the same as that course without the P after it. We spend most of the first day of class explaining to students that they are in a pilot section and calming their terrified freshman nerves over what that might mean. Some of my colleagues who have not yet taught in the pilot project are uneasy about our emphasis on expressive writing and are concerned that we are lowering standards by not paying so much attention to grammar, usage, punctuation, and spelling. Some who have taught in the pilot program have had difficulty adjusting to the change from an instructor-centered to a student-centered classroom, particularly in using the small-group workshops, which tend to seem rather chaotic and noisy. Some students fear they will not learn as much about grammar as they ought to in these courses. However, students in pilot sections have no greater failure rate on the English 102 exam than do students in the traditional sections, even though the exam is heavily weighted to measure matters of grammar and mechanics. And those instructors who have taught in both the traditional and the pilot program agree that the students have a better attitude toward writing and write much more interesting essays in the pilot sections. In the future, as we formally evaluate the pilot project, we will be able to say more about its successes or failures.

William A. Geiger, Jr.

28. Whittier College Freshman Composition Program

1. **Department responsible for the writing program:** English

2. **Staffing**

Percentage of freshman composition courses taught by part-time faculty members	33%
Percentage taught by full-time instructors	11%
Percentage taught by assistant, associate, and full professors	56%
Percentage taught by full-time members of departments other than English	0%

3. **Enrollment policy**

Maximum enrollment	41
Minimum enrollment	21
Average enrollment	32

4. **Program size**

   Number of students enrolled in the freshman composition program
fall 1984	326
spring 1985	255

   Number of sections of freshman composition offered
fall 1984	9
spring 1985	9

History

Whittier College's freshman English program was originally designed by Albert Upton in the early 1930s. We have used various texts over the years, but two have remained the core of our program: Upton's *Design for Thinking* and Upton, Richard Samson, and Ann Farmer's *Creative Analysis*. *Design for Thinking* presents our theory, and *Creative Analysis* presents a sequence of graded exercises designed to lead our students to a working understanding of semantic concepts, what I. A. Richards would term *"assisted* invitations" to understanding language behavior (111). Supplementary texts we have used have included Ann Berthoff's *Forming/Thinking/Writing,* William Sparke and Clark McKowen's *Montage,* Wallace Anderson and Norman Stageberg's *Introductory Readings on Language,* and John Durham and Paul Zall's *Plain Style.* We have used most of the major handbooks (excluding the excessively prescriptive ones) over the years. We presently use a short handbook I authored in 1984.

Theoretical Assumptions

1. We agree with Ernst Cassirer, Susanne K. Langer, Joseph Barwick, Jerome Bruner, and James Britton that classification, the conscious sorting of things, is the fundamental intellectual act. Thus, Whittier's freshman composition course is based on teaching students to see the crucial importance of classification in human behavior and to improve their ability to classify. In addition to classification, we systematically teach our students to perform two other forms of analysis. The ability to perform all three gives them a method for understanding any concept, because these three sorts of analysis express the three fundamental relations and the six basic questions we can ask.

Form of analysis	Relationship
Classification	Genus-species
Structure analysis	Part-whole
Operation analysis	Stage-operation

Basic questions

Classification: What is this a sort of? What are the sorts of this?

Structure analysis: What is this a part of? What are the parts of this?

Operation analysis: What is this a stage of? What are the stages of this?

2. The doctrine of essential ambiguity or verbal economy is a governing concept in our course. All words have the capacity to develop more than one sense of meaning, and our most important words have multiple meanings. Because of the multiplicity of phenomena and our inability to comprehend all phenomena, we need to give old words new meanings in order to make and negotiate our worlds. A measure of a word's importance is registered in the number of meanings we have given it. Words such as *have, reason, set, order, take, cause, in,* and *form,* for example, have acquired large numbers of meanings because the relations and concepts they symbolize go to the heart of our ability to make meanings, as Ann Berthoff puts it. Curiously enough, though, this last fact is rarely mentioned or taught in most English programs, from kindergarten through graduate school.

3. A composition course for us is obligated to teach students not only how to compose both their minds and their essays but also how to interpret accurately what they see and read. Rhetorically, we place a considerable premium on accuracy of interpretation during the problem-solving and expository stages. Although we do teach students how to write argumentative prose (in the sense of persuasive prose), we prefer exposition to argumentation. First, as Mike Rose ("Remedial" 111) and Malcolm Kiniry and Ellen Strenski of UCLA (191) have noted, most of the writing our students are expected to do in

college is expository rather than argumentative. Second, argumentative writing shares the intellectual bankruptcy of traditional debate: any art that values winning through forceful and logical distortion is no fit art for a civilized human being. Being able to apply the principle of ambiguity, and to resolve the meaning of an ambiguous utterance through the laws of matrix and parsimony, and then to communicate one's understanding in apt words to others are, for us, the signs of a liberally educated person.

4. We agree with Janice Lauer and Linda Flower that competent problem solving is crucial to any composition course. Although we stress it throughout our course, we maintain that problem solving as a complex activity cannot be fruitfully studied until after students have achieved competency at analysis and an awareness of the importance of symbolic ambiguity. Further, we make a distinction between problem solving and exposition. Only after students have set up and solved a problem, whether the problem be solved algorithmically or heuristically, can they confront the separate rhetorical problem of addressing their findings to a particular audience.

General Design

1. Following Ann Berthoff's model, we have our students keep a dialectical notebook for course readings, lab discussions, and stages of essay composing. During the first semester, they write weekly themes ranging in length from single 300-word paragraphs through 750-word themes. The first semester's papers are designed to help students master our fundamental semantic ideas. During the second semester, they write fewer but longer papers. The first third of the second semester continues with essays directed toward understanding semantic theory. The second third consists of several stages of a problem-solving project. Each student is expected to formulate a complex problem, survey the possible problems that the several meanings of the problem's key words might yield, choose which construction or meaning the problem is going to have for him or her, and then collet data cards and classify them prior to solving the original question or problem.

2. Our students compose several sorts of writing. Their journals reflect the reciprocal commerce between what James Britton terms expressive and transactive discourse. As befits the experimental and personal nature of journals, the journals are evaluated for evidence of thinking about the readings and discussions, not for their rhetorical and grammatical competency. Formal papers are graded, however, with less weight being placed on the first themes of the first semester than on later ones. The dominant mode of discourse for the first semester is expository prose. Only after our students have developed the ability to articulate a clear and considered thesis supported by sound evidence do we let them write persuasive or argumentative prose. Persuasive prose is the dominant mode of the second semester's writing. We believe there is sound psychological and pedagogical justification for our order of exposition to persuasion. It is reasonably accurate to assume that most freshmen are both anxious and egocentric. Anxiety is alleviated by giving students an understanding of the tools of thought necessary for constructing accurate accounts of reality. The need to write expository prose forces students to go beyond themselves in a responsible and accountable way. Only after they come to appreciate the need for accuracy can they be allowed to dis-

cuss the merits and limitations of multiple viewpoints, thus going beyond egocentricity. It is better, that is, to be reasonable than "right."

Staffing and Teacher Training

Every full-time (six) and part-time (one to three, depending on our needs) member of our English department is responsible for one section of English composition. Teacher training is formally handled in two ways. First, the entire staff (together with our student discussion leaders) meets each week for an afternoon meeting during which we discuss the course content and assignments for the following week. The new faculty members are invited to participate in the meeting, but no pressure is placed on them if they choose to observe rather than take a leading role. The burden of conducting the meeting is placed primarily on the long-time faculty members. Second, the new members frequently attend seasoned faculty members' lectures. Our informal methods of teacher training include visiting with faculty members to discuss pedagogical and subject-matter questions.

Our student discussion leaders are junior and senior students who did well in English composition (a grade of B or better), who have been recommended for the position by their teachers, and who chose to accept an invitation to lead a discussion section. Before students can lead a discussion group on semantic theory, they must enroll in a four-unit preparatory course taught by the director of the program. It is important to realize that these student discussion leaders are *not* faculty members. Their primary responsibility is to lead discussion groups of ten to twelve students; they do not evaluate papers or examinations. Most of our discussion leaders live on campus; consequently, many freshmen visit the coaches for assistance in brainstorming and for reading rough drafts. The use of student discussion leaders began with a practical necessity: some way had to be found to conduct a responsible program for the large influx of veterans after World War II without appreciably increasing our faculty size. We soon found (and have had our conclusion verified since that time) that using student discussion leaders is one of our program's strengths. Our freshmen are less reluctant to offer ideas (including "wrong" ones) to a peer than to a superior. A highly desirable by-product of our coaching system is that most Whittier College graduates who have been discussion leaders and who have become teachers have generally been superior teachers in our public and private schools, ranging from kindergarten through college; those who have entered other professions have made strong use of their ability to engage in productive and thoughtful discussion and to analyze and solve problems.

Problems

1. A major recent problem was solved last year. During 1982-84 we had large team-taught classes, ranging in size from 80 to 105 students. The classes met as a whole only for lectures, and the majority of class time was devoted to small discussion groups (ten to thirteen students per section). The paper grading was handled by the two teachers plus one reader per section. We decided

that the large lectures were incompatible with a small college, so last year we attempted to limit our classes to thirty students per section—positive student evaluations of our course increased dramatically.

2. A second major problem is an abiding one. Because most of our faculty members had traditional freshman composition programs when they were freshmen, most criticisms of our program are based on the premises and practices of these traditional courses. We have thus encountered all the problems noted by Stephen Judy and Susan Judy: criticisms of English programs based on uncritical personal experience, unsound pedagogy, and the assumption that any person has the right to criticize an English composition program because English composition is not viewed as a subject having its own methods, theory, and findings (3). Our strongest critics have sought to change our program from a complex liberal arts perspective to a concern for "writing skills" detached from the larger issues of responsible analysis and interpretation. We concur with Thomas R. Whitaker that we as English professors teach "reading and writing—which is to say, interpretation" and that our goal as English professors in this decade is not "to capitulate to the crudest assumptions of the marketplace, . . . [but] to reinterpret . . . what it should mean for us to be teachers of interpretation" (1).

3. Budgets are a frequent problem for us. Last year, for example, an attempt was made to cut out all part-time help and most of our student discussion leaders for the English department for 1985-86, despite the demonstrated need for part-time faculty and the overwhelming success of our discussion-leader program over the years. Whittier already has two to four fewer full-time department members than other local colleges (Occidental and Pomona); cutting out part-time help and our discussion leaders would seriously damage our program.

Strengths

1. We have a coherent program based on a psychologically sound pattern of cognitive development, expressed in a few sequential interlocking concepts, a core set of ideas arranged hierarchically that manifest Jerome Bruner's concept of a "spiral curriculum" (52-54).

2. Our program has the advantage of being both traditional (for us) and innovative. Although its superstructure was laid about fifty years ago, we have consistently introduced new ideas, generated new approaches, discarded unsatisfactory ideas, and brought to bear sound psychological and pedagogical ideas from recognized authorities. Insights drawn from Ernst Cassirer, Susanne K. Langer, James Britton, Ann Berthoff, and Jerome Bruner, to name only a few people, complement and enrich our fundamental structure, gained from C. K. Ogden and I. A. Richards as formulated by Albert Upton. According to Ann Berthoff, Francis Crick once observed that you know when a conceptual model works because "you get more out of it than you . . . put in" (Berthoff, *Making* 7). Crick's observation sums up our attitude toward our course.

3. The use of qualified and trained upper-division student discussion leaders has been an abiding strength of our program for almost forty years. Not only do our students profit from having peers to assist them in mastering

semantic theory, but the number of former discussion leaders who have gone on to positions in business, education, the law, and other occupations and professions have done so with greater confidence in being able to participate in and lead discussions and to analyze and solve problems.

4. The utility of our analytic techniques in other courses and in business and professional work has long been a source of satisfaction to us. Countless graduates over the past fifty years have noted the utility and importance of our program in their lives.

Works Cited

Anaya, Rudolfo. *Bless Me, Ultima*. Berkeley: Tonatiuh, 1976.

Anderson, Wallace L., and Norman Stageberg, eds. *Introductory Readings on Language*. 4th ed. New York: Holt, 1975.

Applebee, Arthur. *Writing in the Secondary School: English and the Content Areas*. Urbana: NCTE, 1981.

Bailey, Richard. "This Teaching Works: The English Composition Board of the University of Michigan." Report to the Coll. of Literature, Science, and the Arts, U of Michigan, Ann Arbor, Aug. 1981.

Barry, Lois. "The Busy Professor's Guide to Writing across the Curriculum." Unpublished pamphlet. Eastern Oregon Stage C.

Barry, Vincent. *Good Reason for Writing: A Text with Readings*. Belmont: Wadsworth, 1982.

Bazerman, Charles. *The Informed Writer*. Boston: Houghton, 1981.

———. "A Relationship between Reading and Writing: The Conversational Model." *College English* 41 (1980): 656–61.

Behrens, Laurence, and Leonard Rosen. *Writing and Reading across the Curriculum*. Boston: Little, 1982.

Berke, Jacqueline. *Twenty Questions for the Writer: A Rhetoric with Readings*. 3rd ed. New York: Harcourt, 1981.

Berthoff, Ann E. *Forming/Thinking/Writing: The Composing Imagination*. Upper Montclair: Boynton, 1982.

———. *The Making of Meaning: Metaphors, Models, and Maxims for Writing Teachers*. Upper Montclair: Boynton, 1981.

Bloom, Benjamin S. *Human Characteristics and School Learning*. New York: McGraw, 1976.

Bolker, Joan. "Reflections on Reading Student Writing." *College English* 39 (1978): 181–85.

Booth, Wayne C. *Critical Understanding: The Powers and Limits of Pluralism*. Chicago: U of Chicago P, 1979.

———. *Modern Dogma and the Rhetoric of Assent*. Chicago: U of Chicago P, 1974.

Boyer, Ernest L. *High School: A Report on Secondary Education in America*. New York: Harper, 1983.

Britton, James. *The Development of Writing Abilities, 11–18*. School Council Research Studies. London: Macmillan; Urbana: NCTE, 1975.

Bruffee, Kenneth A. "Collaborative Learning and 'The Conversation of Mankind.'" *College English* 46 (1984): 635–52.

———. "The Developmental Education Program: A Conceptual Analysis." Unpublished pamphlet. Brooklyn: Brooklyn C, 1979.

———. *A Short Course in Writing*. 2nd ed. Boston: Little, 1980.

Bruner, Jerome S. *The Process of Education*. Cambridge: Harvard UP, 1961.

Burhans, Clinton S., Jr. "The Teaching of Writing and the Knowledge Gap." *College English* 45 (1983): 639–56.

Burke, Kenneth. *Language as Symbolic Action: Essays on Life, Literature, and Method*. Berkeley: U of California P, 1966.

CBS Reports. *Blacks in America: "With All Deliberate Speed"?* Narr. Ed Bradley. WCBS, New York. 17 May 1979.

Charmey, Davida. "The Validity of Using Holistic Scoring to Evaluate Writing: A Critical Overview." *Research in the Teaching of English* 18 (1984): 65-81.

Coles, William E., Jr. *Composing: Writing as a Self-Creating Process.* Rochelle Park: Hayden, 1974.

———. *Teaching Composing.* Upper Montclair: Boynton, 1974.

Comley, Nancy R., et al., eds. *Fields of Writing: Readings across the Disciplines.* New York: St. Martin's, 1984.

Cooper, Charles, ed. *The Nature and Measurement of Competency in English.* Urbana: NCTE, 1981.

Corbett, Edward P. J. *The Little English Handbook: Choices and Conventions.* 4th ed. Glenview: Scott, 1984.

Daiker, Donald, Andrew Kerek, and Max Morenberg. *The Writer's Options: Combining to Composing.* 2nd ed. New York: Harper, 1982.

D'Angelo, Frank. *Process and Thought in Composition.* 2nd ed. Boston: Little, 1980.

Dawe, Charles W., et al. *One to One: Resources for Conference-Centered Writing.* 2nd ed. Boston: Little, 1984.

Day, Susan, and Elizabeth McMahan. *The Writer's Resource: Readings for Composition.* New York: McGraw, 1983.

Durham, John, and Paul Zall. *Plain Style.* New York: McGraw, 1967.

Eastman, Arthur M., et al., eds. *The Norton Reader.* 6th ed. New York: Norton, 1983.

Elbow, Peter. "Embracing Contraries in the Teaching Process." *College English* 45 (1983): 327-39.

———. "Trying to Teach While Thinking about the End." Grant et al. 95-137.

———. *Writing with Power: Techniques for Mastering the Writing Process.* New York: Oxford UP, 1981.

———. *Writing without Teachers.* New York: Oxford UP, 1973.

Emig, Janet. *The Composing Processes of Twelfth Graders.* Urbana: NCTE, 1971.

———. *The Web of Meaning: Essays on Writing, Teaching, Learning, and Thinking.* Upper Montclair: Boynton, 1983.

Erikson, Erik. *Childhood and Society.* 2nd ed. New York: Norton, 1963.

Fish, Stanley. *Is There a Text in This Class? The Authority of Interpretive Communities.* Cambridge: Harvard UP, 1980.

Flower, Linda. "A Cognitive Process Theory of Writing." *College Composition and Communication* 32 (1981): 365-87.

———. *Problem-Solving Strategies for Writing.* New York: Harcourt, 1981.

———. "Writer-Based Prose: A Cognitive Basis for Problems in Writing." *College English* 41 (1979): 19-37.

Flynn, James, and Joseph Glaser. *A Writer's Handbook.* New York: Macmillan, 1984.

Fulwiler, Toby. "Writing as an Act of Cognition." *Teaching Writing in All Disciplines.* Ed. C. Williams Griffin. San Francisco: Jossey, 1982. 15-26.

Fulwiler, Toby, and Art Young, eds. *Language Connections: Writing and Reading across the Curriculum.* Urbana: NCTE, 1982.

Garrison, Roger. *How a Writer Works.* New York: Harper, 1981.

Geertz, Clifford. *The Interpretation of Cultures.* New York: Basic, 1973.

———. *Local Knowledge: Further Essays in Interpretive Anthropology.* New York: Basic, 1983.

Gefvert, Constance J. *The Confident Writer.* New York: Norton, 1985.

Gibaldi, Joseph, and Walter S. Achtert. *MLA Handbook for Writers of Research Papers.* 2nd ed. New York: MLA, 1984.

Gorell, Donna. "Toward Determining a Minimal Competency: Entrance Examination for Freshman Composition." *Research in the Teaching of English* 17 (1983): 263–74.

Grant, Gerald, et al., eds. *On Competence: A Critical Analysis of Competence-Based Reforms in Higher Education.* San Francisco: Jossey, 1979.

Graves, Donald. *Balance the Basics: Let Them Write.* New York: Ford Foundation, 1978.

———. *Writing: Teachers and Children at Work.* Exeter: Heinemann, 1982.

Heath, Shirley B. *Ways with Words: Language, Life, and Work in Communities and Classrooms.* New York: Cambridge UP, 1983.

Hirsch, E. D. *The Philosophy of Composition.* Chicago: U of Chicago P, 1977.

Hodges, John C., and Mary E. Whitten. *Harbrace College Handbook.* 9th ed. New York: Harcourt, 1984.

Irmscher, William. *Teaching Expository Writing.* New York: Holt, 1979.

Iser, Wolfgang. *The Act of Reading: A Theory of Aesthetic Response.* Baltimore: Johns Hopkins UP, 1979.

Jacobus, Lee A., ed. *A World of Ideas: Essential Readings for College Writers.* New York: St. Martin's, 1983.

Johnson, Robert A. *He: Understanding Masculine Psychology.* New York: Harper, 1977.

Judy, Stephen N., and Susan J. Judy. *An Introduction to the Teaching of Writing.* New York: Wiley, 1981.

Kane, Thomas S. *The Oxford Guide to Writing.* Ed. Nancy Sommers. New York: Oxford UP, 1984.

Keizer, Mervyn, et al. *The Developmental Education Program, Brooklyn College: A Conceptual Synthesis.* Unpublished report, 1979.

Kennedy, X. J. *Literature: An Introduction to Fiction, Poetry, and Drama.* 3rd ed. Boston: Little, 1983.

Kiniry, Malcolm, and Ellen Strensky. "Sequencing Expository Writing: A Recursive Approach." *College Composition and Communication* 36 (1985): 191–202.

Kinneavy, James. *Theory of Discourse.* New York: Norton, 1980.

Kolbenschlag, Madonna. *Kiss Sleeping Beauty Good-bye: Breaking the Spell of Feminine Myths and Models.* New York: Doubleday, 1979.

Krupa, Gene. *Situational Writing.* Belmont: Wadsworth, 1982.

Kuhn, Thomas S. *The Structure of Scientific Revolutions.* 2nd ed. Chicago: U of Chicago P, 1970.

Lambert, Wallace E. *Language, Psychology, and Culture.* Stanford: Stanford UP, 1972.

Langer, Susanne K. *Mind: An Essay on Human Feeling.* 3 vols. Baltimore: Johns Hopkins UP, 1967–82.

Lauer, Janice M., et al. *The Four Worlds of Writing.* 2nd ed. New York: Harper, 1985.

Leggett, Glenn, C. David Mead, and William Charvat. *Prentice-Hall Handbook for Writers.* 8th ed. Englewood Cliffs: Prentice, 1982.

Litzinger, Boyd. *The Heath Reader.* Lexington: Heath, 1983.

Macrorie, Ken. *Searching Writing.* Upper Montclair: Boynton, 1980.

———. *Telling Writing.* 3rd ed. Upper Montclair: Boynton, 1980.

Maimon, Elaine, et al. *Readings in the Arts and Sciences.* Boston: Little, 1984.

———. *Writing in the Arts and Sciences.* Boston: Little, 1981.

Malcolm X. *The Autobiography of Malcolm X.* 1965. New York: Ballantine, 1977.

Martin, Nancy. *Writing and Learning across the Curriculum, 11–16.* Upper Montclair: Boynton, 1979.

McClelland, D. C. "Testing for Competence Rather Than for Intelligence." *American Psychologist* 28 (1973): 1–14.

McMahan, Elizabeth, and Susan Day. *The Writer's Rhetoric and Handbook*. New York: McGraw, 1984.

Moffett, James. *Active Voice: A Writing Program across the Curriculum*. Upper Montclair: Boynton, 1981.

———. *Coming on Center: English Education in Evolution*. Upper Montclair: Boynton, 1981.

———. *Teaching the Universe of Discourse*. New York: Houghton, 1982.

Moss, Andrew, and Carol Holder. *Improving Student Writing: A Guidebook for Faculty in All Disciplines*. Pomona: California State Polytechnic U, 1982.

Murray, Donald. *Learning by Teaching: Selected Articles on Writing and Teaching*. Upper Montclair: Boynton, 1982.

———. *A Writer Teaches Writing*. New York: Houghton, 1968.

———. *Write to Learn*. New York: Holt, 1984.

Muscatine, Charles, and Marlene Griffith, eds. *The Borzoi College Reader*. 5th ed. New York: Knopf, 1983.

Neel, Jasper, ed. *Options for the Teaching of English: Freshman Composition*. Options for Teaching 2. New York: MLA, 1978.

Odell, Lee. *Research on Composing: Points of Departure*. Urbana: NCTE, 1978.

Odell, Lee, and Charles Cooper, eds. *Evaluating Writing: Describing, Measuring, Judging*. Urbana: NCTE, 1977.

Oestereicher, Mary. "Student Assessment and Program Evaluation in Brooklyn College's Developmental Education Program." *Doxa* 2.3 (1984): 1–3. ERIC ED 248 737.

Ong, Walter J. *Interfaces of the Word: Studies in the Evolution of Consciousness and Culture*. Ithaca: Cornell UP, 1977.

———. *Orality and Literacy: The Technologizing of the Word*. New York: Methuen, 1982.

Pearce, Roy Harvey, ed. *Savagism and Civilization: A Study of the Indian and the American Mind*. Baltimore: Johns Hopkins UP, 1967.

Pelz, Karen. *Exploratory Writing*. Dubuque: Kendall, 1984.

Perl, Sondra. "Understanding Composing." *College Composition and Communication* 31 (1981): 363–69.

Perrin, Noel. "What This Country Needs Is a Melt Down." *New York Times* 20 Aug. 1983.

Raines, Ann. *Focus on Composition*. New York: Oxford UP, 1978.

Richards, I. A. *Design for Escape*. New York: Harcourt, 1968.

Rorty, Richard. *Philosophy and the Mirror of Nature*. Princeton: Princeton UP, 1979.

Rose, Mike. "Remedial Writing Courses: A Critique and a Proposal." *College English* 45 (1983): 109–28.

———. "Rigid Rules, Inflexible Plans, and the Stifling of Language: A Cognitivist Analysis of Writer's Block." *College Composition and Communication* 30 (1980): 389–401.

———. *Writer's Block: The Cognitive Dimension*. Studies in Writing and Rhetoric. Carbondale: Southern Illinois UP, 1983.

Rosenblatt, Louise. *The Reader, the Text, the Poem: The Transactional Theory of the Literary Work*. Carbondale: Southern Illinois UP, 1978.

Schell, Jonathan. *The Fate of the Earth*. New York: Knopf, 1982.

Scholes, Robert. *Fabulation and Metafiction.* Champaign: U of Illinois P, 1979.

———. *Semiotics and Interpretation.* New Haven: Yale UP, 1981.

Shaughnessy, Mina. *Errors and Expectations: A Guide for the Teacher of Basic Writing.* New York: Oxford UP, 1977.

Shaw, Harry. *A Complete Course in Freshman English.* 8th ed. New York: Harper, 1979.

Sheils, M. "Why Johnny Can't Write." *Newsweek* 8 Dec. 1975: 58-62.

Shrodes, Caroline, et al. *The Conscious Reader.* 2nd ed. New York: Macmillan, 1978.

Smith, Charles K. *Styles and Structures: Alternative Approaches to College Writing.* New York: Norton, 1974.

Sommers, Nancy, and Donald McQuade, eds. *Student Writers at Work.* New York: St. Martin's, 1983.

Sparke, William, and Clark McKowen. *Montage: Investigations in Language.* New York: Macmillan, 1970.

Stanford, Gene. *How to Handle the Paper Load.* Urbana: NCTE, 1979.

Sternglass, Marilyn S. *Reading, Writing, and Reasoning.* New York: Macmillan, 1983.

Strong, William. *Sentence Combining: A Composing Book.* 2nd ed. New York: Random, 1983.

Strunk, William, Jr., and E. B. White. *The Elements of Style.* 3rd ed. New York: Macmillan, 1979.

Stubbs, Marcia, and Sylvan Barnet, eds. *The Little, Brown Reader.* 3rd ed. Boston: Little, 1983.

Taylor, Pat. "Teaching Creativity in Argumentation." *College English* 38 (1977): 507-10.

Upton, Albert. *Design for Thinking: A First Book in Semantics.* Rev. ed. Palo Alto: Pacific, 1973.

Upton, Albert, Richard Samson, and Ann Farmer. *Creative Analysis.* Rev. ed. New York: Dutton, 1978.

Vygotsky, Lev S. *Thought and Language.* Ed. Gertrude Vakar. Trans. Eugenia Hanfmann. Cambridge: MIT P, 1962.

Wasson, John M. *Subject and Structure: An Anthology for Writers.* 8th ed. Boston: Little, 1984.

Watkins, Floyd C., and William B. Dillingham. *Practical English Handbook.* 6th ed. Boston: Houghton, 1982.

Weiss, Robert, and John P. Field. *Cases in Composition.* 2nd ed. Boston: Little, 1984.

Whitaker, Thomas R. "Conversation as Design." *Profession 84.* New York: MLA, 1984. 1-4.

Williams, Joseph M. *Origins of the English Language: A Social and Linguistic History.* New York: Free, 1975.

Young, Richard E., Alton L. Becker, and Kenneth L. Pike. *Rhetoric: Discovery and Change.* New York: Harcourt, 1970.

Zinsser, William. *On Writing Well: An Informal Guide to Writing Nonfiction.* New York: Harper, 1980.

Topical Index

Collaborative learning, 3, 7, 13, 43–45, 50, 57, 81–82, 100–01
Computers/word processing, 55, 88
Conferences, 19, 23, 43–45, 59, 80
Course descriptions, 7–8, 13–14, 18–19, 22–23, 26–27, 31, 33–37, 40–41, 60–61, 65–66, 68–70, 71–74, 76–78, 83–84, 86–87, 90–93, 107–09, 112–14, 120, 123, 125–26, 140–41, 144–45, 150–51, 157–58
Developmental/remedial courses and programs, 3, 16–17, 20, 35, 42, 49–50, 57–58, 73–74, 82, 113, 136
Evaluation/grading of writing, 8, 19, 21–22, 58, 63, 67, 78, 94, 95–96, 99–100, 102–03
Interdisciplinary approaches, 8, 14, 27, 29, 31, 41, 46, 49, 52, 73, 84, 143
Peer tutoring, 4, 8–9, 23–25, 58, 61–62, 107
Placement/exemption policies, 3, 13, 34–35, 50, 83, 105, 112, 119
Problems and strengths of programs, 9–11, 20, 28, 38–39, 55–56, 63–64, 66, 67–68, 74–75, 93–94, 103–05, 109–10, 115–16, 128, 134, 141–42, 146–47, 153–54, 158–59
Proficiency/exit examinations, 4, 32, 33–35, 38, 58–59, 66, 74, 77, 85, 86, 96–97, 107
Reading-writing connections, 8, 18, 27–28, 30, 50–51, 65–67, 73, 78–79, 86, 152
School-college cooperation, 4, 11, 15, 46, 49–51, 80, 110, 119
Staff: training, development, preparation, 3, 9, 22, 24, 28, 32, 37, 42, 46, 50, 54, 61–62, 68, 78, 84, 87, 107, 114–15, 127–28, 133–34, 141, 145–46, 153, 158
Theoretical assumptions, 2, 7, 12–13, 17–18, 27, 30–31, 35, 41–43, 50–51, 59–60, 66–67, 72, 81, 108–09, 112, 121, 123–24, 132–33, 135, 156–58
Writing across the curriculum, 3, 8, 13–14, 18, 22–23, 34, 38, 41, 45–46, 49, 52–53, 72–73, 81–82
Writing centers, 4, 14, 23, 41–42, 43, 49, 54, 84, 107, 120–21
Writing-intensive courses and programs, 7, 23, 38, 49, 65–67, 84